Africa at the Crossroads

CHRISTIAN PERSPECTIVES
ON SOCIAL PROBLEMS

Gayraud S. Wilmore, *General Editor*

Africa
at the
Crossroads

by

JAMES H. ROBINSON

Philadelphia
THE WESTMINSTER PRESS

LIBRARY OF CONGRESS CATALOG CARD NO. 62–17810

PRINTED IN THE UNITED STATES OF AMERICA

N 1 0 6

Contents

Foreword

THIS BOOK IS ONE OF SEVERAL TO APPEAR DURING THE
next few years in a series entitled Christian Perspectives
on Social Problems. This is an attempt to meet a challenge
from an exceedingly robust minority of laymen for brief,
readable analyses of cultural problems from a theological
perspective. It is intended to help them *think theologically*
about some of the exasperatingly difficult problems of
society, both the issues relating to life in America and
those linking this nation to the destiny of the world.

Recent researches on family life have found laymen
obsessed with "loving, happy relations" in the family,
with child-rearing and personal problems of status and
adjustment, but with little comprehension of how private
troubles bisect public issues. This curious fascination with
selfhood to the neglect of neighborhood is not, however,
a universal malaise of Protestantism. A minority, perhaps, but a minority that refuses to be lightly regarded
by ecclesiastical officialdom, is demanding to know the
meaning of events of our day for the Christian faith
and to demonstrate the critical and renewing power of
faith in secular society.

It is to these doughty men and women that the several
volumes of the Christian Perspectives on Social Problems series are directed, and it is hoped that they not only
will make for an unsettling reading experience but will

1

provide stimulating material for small-group study and discussion. To that end, questions for discussion are appended to each of the books as starters for fruitful controversy.

Christian action in foreign affairs has conventionally identified the underdeveloped areas, particularly Africa, as one of the great social and cultural problems of the modern world. The significance of this contribution to the Christian Perspectives on Social Problems series is that it reverses this point of view. It is not Africa but America and American Christianity that is a problem to the redemptive activity of God in the world today.

AFRICA AT THE CROSSROADS is a summons and a strategy for *emergent Americans,* to use the title of Harold R. Isaac's report on Dr. Robinson's internationally famous Operation Crossroads Africa. It diagnoses the problem of the unprofitable relations which have, until recently, obtained between the people of the United States and the peoples of Africa and other areas formerly under colonial domination. It calls for a new policy by which Americans can emerge as responsible citizens of a world to which claim is being laid today by Asians and Africans.

James H. Robinson, as many readers will know, organized and directs the project Operation Crossroads Africa, which since 1958 has taken more than seven hundred young people into Africa on a mission of friendship across national, racial, and cultural barriers. The present volume is intimately connected with the experiences and insights that have derived from the Crossroads venture. It points the way to more effective outreach, both in Christian missions and American foreign policy, through the kind of sharing and "people to people" diplomacy that lifts international relations to a new and creative dimension.

GAYRAUD S. WILMORE

Pittsburgh, Pennsylvania

Chapter I

The New Perspective on Africa

MODERN AFRICA STANDS AT THE CROSSROADS OF HIStory, shedding an old order encrusted with ancient customs and passing through the crisis of rebirth and renewal. This remarkable land—the continent of the future—has been a far more significant and important focal point for Europe and the Middle East, for the subcontinent of India for at least a hundred years, and for the United States during the last half century than most people have realized. Only our present awareness of its rapid and convulsive changes, which move so fast that even a week in Africa is a long time, is new. The intrusion of outsiders, the exploitation of its mineral resources, the enslavement of its people, the division and control of its land, and the ignorance on our part of its finer development and noblest achievements are old.

The events shaping up in modern Africa can no longer be ignored. They are of vital and direct concern to us, morally, politically, economically, and socially, as well as ideologically. The historical forces, midwifing the birth of new Africa, are moving faster than Westerners, the rest of the world, or perhaps even the Africans themselves have yet realized. Nevertheless, as the recent series of crises in developing Africa have demonstrated, both our destiny and our future will be powerfully influenced by what happens in Africa. We simply cannot under-

3

stand the demands of Africa's hour of crisis and what they
ultimately portend for us unless our thinking is shaped
within the context of its past in order that we may
remove the darkness from our hearts, the ignorance from
our minds, and the condescension in our attitudes. The
point of the beginning is therefore not with the crises
of the moment but with the history of the past.

I

The continent of Africa is more than five thousand
miles long from north to south and just short of four
thousand miles wide from east to west. Its total coast
line is 3,500 miles longer than half the circumference
of the earth. As a land mass of 11,250,000 square miles,
it is nearly three and one half times the size of the United
States, more than twice the size of Europe and the
Middle East combined. The 200,000,000 people who
populate the continent speak a bewildering number of
separate languages and dialects. However, English and
French have become the two main channels of communication, not only for the educated but increasingly for
those who have had little or no education. Thus English
and French have become the modern *lingua franca,* with
Portuguese and Afrikaans in a limited and very minor
role.

Africa's races include the great mass of Negroid peoples, such as the Hottentots, Zulus, and Bantus in South
Africa; the Hausas, Mandingos, Yorubas, Fantis, Bafas,
Ibos, Ashantis; the Kikuyu, Watusi, Masai, and Matabali
in East and Central Africa; and many, many other
smaller tribal groups with whose names we have recently
become familiar in Guinea, the Cameroons, Angola, the
Congo, and Kenya. There are also the Berbers in the
eastern part of North Africa, the Arabs and the Fulanese,
the Indians and Pakistanis in East, Central, and South

Africa, the Greeks and Lebanese in West Africa, and the Europeans from England, France, Holland, Spain, and Portugal who have taken up permanent residence in those areas where the climatic conditions have been conducive to establishing settlements and where business and industrial opportunities have demanded their presence. Africa is not, as so many Americans have assumed, one great, big, black blob of similar Negroid people. Its social customs, religious institutions, modes of dress, and the relationship of its people to time and eternity is as varied and different as its colors, its languages, its tribal groupings and races.

The paths of Europeans who began the first probing penetration of Africa along its coast began before the Christian Era. Recent historical studies have shown that in ancient times many ventured much farther into its brooding interior than the fringes of the coast line. Such discoveries have confirmed ancient Greek writers who alluded to contact and relationships of African people with the outside world many hundreds of years before Christ. The relationship between Israel and Ethiopia is but one case in point. Penetration by Christian forces began in the first century of the Christian Era and flowered and reached its high-water mark in the second and third centuries, chiefly along the coast of North Africa and in Ethiopia. During the life-and-death struggles of Western Europe with the Goths and later with fiery forces of Islam's conquest of North Africa, the Christian roots withered in North Africa and were separated from the main stream in Ethiopia where they were isolated.

After consolidating its gains along the Mediterranean coast, Islam began its southward march across the Sahara. By the ninth century it had laid the foundations of great empires, of Songay, Mali, Meli, and Ghana. During the following three hundred years until the twelfth century these empires reached a high degree of civilization, political organization, and culture. For example, the kingdoms of the Ashantis in Ghana and the Benin in Nigeria were well developed, highly organized, and the most powerful areas along the west coast of Africa long before the advent of the Europeans. They were rich in oral tradition and material artifacts revealing a superb degree of artistry and technical skill in their works of bronze, ivory, wood, iron, brass, pottery, and cloth. Their emissaries and ambassadors spread out along the whole coast of Africa, and some of them were not unknown in Spain and Portugal.

But the concentrated, continuous penetration of Africa did not begin until the fourteenth century. Henry IV, of Portugal, an intrepid explorer, personally led many expeditions to North Africa and for a considerable way down the coast of West Africa. He was impelled by gold and trade, but also by a desire to find Prester John, rumored to be a fabulous king in East Africa, with whom he could make an alliance to help hold back the tide of the Moslem penetration. His sailors developed contacts along the west coast down as far as the Congo River, and one of his emissaries, in the same year that Columbus discovered the Americas, traversed the land mass of Africa in search of Prester John, until he reached an area we know now to be ancient Ethiopia. The success of the Portuguese explorers and merchants was followed by that of the French, the British, and the Danes in their frantic search that developed into a violent struggle for trade and territory. The Arabs in the Middle East had already begun to establish their foothold on the eastern coast of Africa and had for centuries dealt in the chattel slavery of African peoples.

II

With the discovery of the Western hemisphere and the colonization of the United States, slavery, which had long been a lucrative business in East Africa and not unknown even among the African tribes themselves, became an equally lucrative business to supply urgently needed labor for the New World. Thus from the very beginning of its history the United States has been involved in Africa, unfortunately in a most unhappy way. Slavery in a democracy is a festering paradox that contaminates the whole body politic and despoils both the slave and the slaver. As the Secretary of the Treasury of Liberia, who is also President of the International Council of the Y.M.C.A., once said, "Few periods in men's existence have seen such diabolical debasement of the human person and the demoralization of Africa which came as a result of the slave trade." We can be sure, however, that for every slave who survived his capture, incarceration, the middle voyage, and his first few years in the United States, four to five lost their lives in the process. Some authorities suggest that the ratio was even higher. The brutal slave trade that ravaged and convulsed in a slaughter too staggering for human conscience to grasp is a blot on America for which we owe a debt that we can never fully repay to the people of Africa. We have not yet fully contemplated either the degradation to which it dragged us down before emancipation or the guilt complexes that operate unconsciously in our minds because of it up to this day.

From the beginning of the slave trade, there were a few courageous souls in the United States who could not square their nation's indulgence in chattel slavery with their Christian conscience and religious idealism. What they lacked in numbers and influence, they made up in vigor and zeal as they battled against the powerful forces that tried to justify turning human personalities into commodities.

The Quakers, among the first to oppose the institution of slavery, were joined by many others until at one time there were more than five hundred antislavery societies across the nation. Most of them suffered abuse, brutality, and jailings, and some of the Quakers were accused of treason in more than one session of Congress. But their persistence enlarged their forces until they were strong enough to tackle the ambivalent, Yankee, Bible-quoting shippers and the cultured Southern plantation owners, who tried to erase the nightmare from their consciences by arguing that the slave was less than a man, had only second-rate potentialities for the Kingdom of Heaven, and was worth no more than three fifths of a citizen in the American commonwealth. Their efforts began to bear fruit, for the aroused and troubled conscience of American citizens was gradually able to bring the Government to outlaw slavery as the British had done previously under the indefatigable leadership of Granville Sharpe and William Wilberforce. The work of the latter for the defeat and destruction of the slave trade earned him the epitaph on his grave in Westminster Abbey: "Here lies the Attorney General of the disinherited, the outcast, and the slave." Thomas Jefferson fell early under the influence of these courageous souls and was one of their strongest supporters. Their offspring went on to inspire Robert Lovejoy, Frederick Douglass, William Lloyd Garrison, Sojourner Truth, and Harriet Tubman, who were among the mainstays of the abolitionist movement that finally resulted in the Emancipation Proclamation by President Abraham Lincoln.

Thus our first relationship with the African continent in this country began in a miserable and dishonorable way. From the end of the slave trade and within twenty-five years, there were between three and four hundred thousand freedmen in the United States, most of whom were in the North and not an inconsiderable number in eastern Canada. Although freed from chattel slavery, their lot was little better economically, socially, and politically because they found it exceedingly difficult to be integrated into American society. An attempt was therefore made on the part of a number of groups in the United States to follow the British experience of supporting a back-to-Africa movement that resulted in the founding of Sierra Leone, with its capital appropriately named Freetown.

Earlier, Thomas Jefferson had been interested in the British experiment, and after sending emissaries, asked for permission for manumitted Negro Americans to be admitted to that colony. The first group left in 1815 and a further group went in 1820, under the auspices of the American Missionary Association in New England.

However, only a few hundred ex-slaves were ever returned to Africa chiefly because the colonial powers, which had long controlled the coastal settlements and were beginning to penetrate deeper and deeper into the continent, were both suspicious of, and hostile to, American philanthropic and religious societies intent upon the relocation of freed slaves to their former homeland. By 1830 there were almost none returning, but the remnant founded Liberia. Despite the pitiful way America ignored its heroic struggle to survive, especially against the colonial powers, Liberia has nonetheless remained America's firmest friend in Africa.

The growing economic success of the Portuguese and British establishments, together with the discovery of gold and many other raw materials demanded by the heightening industrial revolution in Europe and European trade with the New World, was followed with a renewed intensity of colonization by the Dutch, the Spanish, the Danes, the French, and lastly, the Germans. Therefore what had been a race for coastal ports and footholds along the coast line became a desperate and frantic struggle for the division of Africa's massive territory and unlimited resources of mineral and commercial wealth.

III

King Leopold II, of Belgium, in 1876 called representatives of Great Britain, Belgium, France, Germany, Austria, Hungary, Italy, and Russia to Brussels to a conference organized for the purpose of determining the best methods of European co-operation and exploitation of the colonies in Africa. But the lure of profits had been too great and the rifts too great. The agreements were never effected to curb the rivalry and desire for control of Africa's wealth. After three years Leopold in 1879 obtained the services of Henry M. Stanley, perhaps the only man who, although not an American citizen, fought on both sides of our Civil War. Leopold sent him to the Congo on a trip of exploration. Stanley, the only white man in the party who survived the expedition across the Congo, sought to give his discovery to Great Britain but was rebuffed. Thus by 1885 Leopold II had under his control 912,000 square miles of some of the richest territory on earth. The area, nearly twice as large as the whole of Western Europe, had Stanley as its first governor and Leopold II as its sole owner. But the area's reputation for brutal treatment of the Africans was so monstrous that the Government debated for a long time when Leopold offered it to the Belgians, and they did not accept it until 1908.

Beginning in the 1840's and continuing through the years of our Civil War, greedy grabs for Africa's soil and soul continued with increased fury until the Berlin conference of November, 1884, to which Austria-Hungary, Belgium, Denmark, France, Great Britain, Holland, Italy, Norway, Portugal, Russia, Spain, Sweden, the United States, and Turkey were invited. It was at this conference that the "spheres of influence" in Africa were established. Arbitrary boundaries were set up, dividing tribal groups in a ruthless fashion; and rules for future occupation, rights to river traffic within the continent, and articles of trade were agreed upon. This was done in an effort to consolidate gains, to end wasteful competition, settle the bloody conflicts, and channel the jealousies and rivalries into more productive economic developments.

During the years of World War I, when the nations of Europe were involved in a life-and-death struggle for survival, their colonies and territories did not escape involvement. Africa was more needed than ever before as a source of supply for materials to feed the industrial machines that were hard pressed to keep up with the consumption of the conflict. The British and French not only recruited African troops for service abroad but trained others to protect their interests in Africa and to enter the war against the Germans. The result was that the latter lost all its colonies in East, West, and Southwest Africa and all of its economic and political influence.

In the two decades between the end of World War I and the beginning of World War II, the European powers concentrated their genius for organization and their industry on the economic development of the resources of Africa with renewed vigor. With the advent of World War II, many more Africans were involved in the conflict on the side of the parent colonial country. At the same time many important military installations were established on the African continent. These were developed chiefly for the purpose of neutralizing General Rommel who commanded the German forces in North Africa. The consequent cross-fertilization of ideas by the buildup of troops from all over the world, including the United States with its large air base in Liberia, together with the return of large numbers of African troops abroad, opened up new vistas to Africa and brought the colonial problem to the focus of world attention. After the war, the first trickle of African students mainly to be trained for posts in the colonial administration began to find its way to the countries of Europe. Although a few were able to come to the United States, chiefly from British-related colonies, most of the European colonies refused to grant them permission to come to this country. But the forces that were born of a burning, smoldering desire for independence, freedom, and equality had achieved more than a toe hold.

It soon became apparent that the colonial powers could no longer ignore the unrest stirring throughout Africa. Perhaps to their surprise, European government officials found among their own citizens a growing dissatisfaction with the inconsistencies of having made great sacrifices for freedom and democracy, then ruthlessly suppressing these same hopes welling up in the minds and hearts of Africans.

Although it prided itself in having no colonies, the United States felt itself being drawn, at first almost imperceptibly but in a few years easily discernibly, into the African involvement. First of all, our allies needed funds desperately to rehabilitate themselves and to maintain their colonies. Foreign loans and foreign aid from the United States supplied those funds. In the second place, our investment capital in Africa increased by over 2,500 per cent in just one decade, from the end of World War II to 1955. Furthermore, our highly technological civilization demanded more and more mineral resources, and Africa was the last great source of the fabulous, untapped resources we needed. We became more and more involved in Africa and in a deeper and more irrevocable way than we realized. Beginning in the early thirties, Africans more and more turned toward the United States, not only for the education and preparation of its sons for future leadership, but because of the faith and confidence of its people in this nation which has had no colonies and had become the professed leader of the democratic world. The presence of that one tenth of the

American population—United States citizens of African descent, the American Negroes—was an added attraction to those Africans whose new world view embraced the Western hemisphere. Africans as long ago as the twenties and thirties seemed to have been more aware of this basis for friendship than either white or black Americans. The United States has had a valuable potential for relationship with Africa that it does not yet appreciate and which many Americans still ignorantly discount.

The Christian forces of the United States continued their work in as large a degree as possible and multiplied their effort by many times between the two wars and after World War II. The work of the churches helped slowly to enlarge the vision and quicken the conscience of Americans and open the eyes of Africans toward the possibilities of the equal human dignity inherent in the gospel the churches taught, even though it was sometimes denied in their relationship to the people they converted. Their work in education and health aroused in Africans not only a sense of the importance of life and an enlargement of their horizons but as well an extension of their lives by the excellent Christian medical work. Until the end of World War II, 90 per cent of all education provided to Africans was made possible by the missionary movement, and until a few years ago, with the exception of the predominantly Moslem countries, almost every African leader received his first education at the hands of Christian missionaries or through the support of Christian churches. Thus the first foundation for leadership in the new Africa was laid by the church and its missionaries.

The whole process toward the change of the centers of power in Africa was accelerated by the Japanese conquest in Asia, even though Japan lost the war in the end. The granting of independence to the Philippines by the United States, the rapid development of independence and freedom in India, Pakistan, Burma, Indonesia, and the restoration of Ethiopia after it fell victim to the unprovoked attack of Mussolini in 1935, also quickened the pace of change in Africa.

Although the European nations were not ready for the events taking shape in Africa, they could no longer ignore the facts of history, nor could the United States continue to plead no responsibility and continue to consider itself innocent of involvement in the tragedy and the hope of Africa. These events conspired to bring Africa to the crossroads of a new historical development and awakening which, in the end, became a revolution that swept the whole continent. Though not clear to some, its end is foreseeable in achieving its goal within the lifetime of the present generation of university and college students. As winner of the Nobel Peace Prize for 1960, Chief Albert John Luthuli, of South Africa, said in his acceptance speech of the award: "The revolution of Africa is a militant struggle for liberty, independence, equality, and human dignity. It is a fight for the right of adult suffrage and the right to stand for and to hold office. . . . This goal pursued by millions of our people with revolutionary zeal, by means of books, representations, demonstrations, and in some places armed force provoked by the intransigency of white rule, carries the only real promise of peace in Africa. Whatever means have been used, the efforts have gone to end alien rule and race oppression."

What the outcome of the revolution will be, no one of us can tell, but it is obligatory upon all of us who believe in freedom, independence, and a peaceful family of nations, living together in mutual respect and co-operation, to work for the best possible solutions and advancement. The revolution will not turn back, and it will not be arrested. Africa at the crossroads of history brings America to the crossroads of some of the most important decisions it will ever have to make, and these decisions will be a part of the future of Africa. They may be the hinges upon which the future of the United States will swing as well.

The directions in which Africa will move from the crossroads of the present will be conditioned and determined by a number of interrelated factors, not the least important of which are the following:

1. How successfully Africans handle the psychological problem of "Who are we, how are we changing, and what do we want most to be?" This is more than a problem of psychology but an even more important philosophical problem of "being."

2. The skill and capacity of African political leadership as it is catapulted into the larger and more exacting demands of wise statesmanship.

3. How patiently and skillfully the peoples of the West will reach out and handle situations when African leadership fails both their peoples and our best hopes; when new power corrupts and blinds some leaders to their democratic responsibilities; and when some leadership becomes authoritarian. This may very likely be the area of the West's greatest testing.

4. How fast sufficient personnel can be trained to take the helm of the basic machinery of Government and also how rapidly the means can be prepared for the elementary functions of an enlightened and responsible citizenship participation.

5. The degree to which progress toward independence in those areas not yet free can be made and how rapidly the forces holding on to positions of preference in these areas will remain impervious to time and change and thus encourage a deepening of despair on the part of Africans, Indians, and Coloreds, while building up hostility and resentment of those countries which have won their freedom.

6. How Pan-Africanism develops co-ordination and co-operation toward effective relationships between new African nations in terms of economic, commercial, and political communications.

7. How well and how gracefully European Government officials and leaders of the settlers can adjust to the implacable demands of African peoples. The essential question is whether or not Europeans have the capacity for leadership that the time demands. Their intransigence can have as negative an effect upon events in Africa as the peaceful change in Tanganyika, Nigeria, and other nations has had positive effect.

8. How rapidly and wisely those who manage, own, and control great industries can help Africans to an equable share of the profits and give them partnership in the direction and control of economic life.

9. How rapidly and effectively the United States can develop and constructively implement its new African policy and how much influence we can bring to bear on our allies; as well as how much assistance we are prepared to give our allies who show a desire to create their own enlightened policies on Africa.

10. The nature and scope of communist aims and the extent and effectiveness of communist strategies. It would be naïve to assume that the communists do not have great aspirations and long-range plans for influencing Africa. Where they are not vigorously at work, they are planning, scheming, confusing, and waiting for the propitious opportunity.

11. Whether the Christian churches in Europe and the Americas, in conjunction with the African churches, can meet the great demands of racial, social, and political change, and whether they can bring the moral imperative of religious responsibility to bear upon their lay representatives who have assumed strategic positions in society.

Whether at this crossroads of history or at some other

in the future, there are two factors of which we can be certain: First, all Africa will obtain its freedom and independence and profoundly influence the destiny of this planet. Second, at some time in the future the present forces shaping the changes in Africa will raise up a new leadership who will lead a second revolution by supplanting the present political leadership. The seeds of revolution, the social and political developments, and the personnel to make this second revolution a reality are apparent and maturing. For example, the National Association of Socialist Student Organizations in Ghana, founded by Ghanaian students in England, has already begun to have a significant impact in Ghana. University student groups in Senegal and Ethiopia also have very definite ideas as to how they would like to run the governments of their countries, as do university students elsewhere in Africa. These students will influence the future, and the future will have to reckon with them. How they react to the challenge, opportunity, and responsibility and who influences them most may well be more important than any combination of present factors.

Chapter II

The Process of Cultural Revolution

I

REVOLUTIONARY CHANGES IN AFRICA ARE SHAKING every social, economic, political, and cultural foundation of that continent from the Mediterranean to the Cape of Good Hope and from Dakar on the west to Zanzibar on the east. These changes, little short of miraculous, have taken place within the last two decades and most of them within the last ten years, but change is not limited to Africa alone. Upheavals have erupted so rapidly in the wake of what Prime Minister Macmillan, of England, called "winds of change" that they have forced the nations of the West, as well as the nations of Asia and the Far East, to make basic readjustments in their attitudes, policies, and strategies with regard to the rapidly developing nations of Africa, nonexistent a half dozen years ago. In the process of these dynamic changes both African nations and African individuals have gained important and increased status as they are thrust by historical circumstances into the family of nations.

At the end of World War II, almost no great nation in the world had any significant plans for relating to what were shortly to be the cataclysmic events of emerging African nations. Most European nations, with the possible exception of Great Britain, still evolved their policies for the areas of Africa they controlled in terms of what they thought would be an indefinite extension of colonial relationships. The United States, at the time, did not even have a desk of any consequence in the Department of State to advise on Africa and obviously had no well-defined African policy. Our policies, if any, were filtered through our colonial allies to the African peoples.

It would also be fair to say that most American Christians thought of Africa in terms of the old Edgar Rice Burroughs frame of reference that considered Africa as a far-off, mysterious, dark continent filled with black, backward, uneducated, uncultured people with no significant history and very little future. This attitude was still prevalent, despite the heroic sacrifice of a significant number of devoted Christians who heard the call of divine mission to share in the redemption of the people of Africa and paid willingly with their lives, knowing that the day they set foot on African soil they would begin to die. It is a sad commentary that few pastors and members of Christian churches in America held to the same degree as these intrepid missionaries from other nations the high hopes of developing a sociological, political, economic, and religious basis for Christianity in Africa.

Up to 1950, all the principal political, economic, and social decisions involving four fifths of the people of Africa and three fourths of its land area were made in London, Paris, Lisbon, and Brussels. It is fortunate for us that these decisions were not made in Washington, although our financial and industrial influence was deeply intertwined in European policy. Unfortunately, on the other hand, we had no influence on the minds of Africans desiring political independence and a new way of life, nor did our Government have any direct international relationships in Africa, except with Liberia, Ethiopia and, to a lesser degree, South Africa. Yet political, economic, and social ferment in Africa had been going on for the last quarter of a century with increasing intensity, even though most of it was submerged since the pleas of Africans were firmly contained, controlled, or suppressed by European powers.

As late as 1958, there were only four African nations, including South Africa, which held membership in the United Nations. Today, there are twenty-five nations, sixteen of which were admitted to the United Nations in 1961. It seems hard to believe, but it is true, that representatives of African nations, along with their Asian colleagues in the Afro-Asian Bloc, now play a very significant, if not dominant role in the United Nations. The result is an entirely new focus on the importance of Africa's role in the world and a radical shift both in the center and in the balance of power.

Until 1959, no African nation, excepting a mere half dozen, had direct relationships of any kind with the countries of the Middle East, Asia, and South America. Almost daily, one reads now of delegations from Africa visiting all parts of the world on political, social, economic, trade, and a variety of other missions. A few years ago there were few, if any, unofficial visitors from Asia and South America to Africa, but today there is scarcely a capital of an independent African country that does not have either accredited diplomatic representatives or plans for future representation to an extent never dreamed of three or four years previously. This is a development of greater significance than most Europeans, Americans, and perhaps even Africans themselves have yet realized. This is precisely so because it brings the African continent into a cross-fertilization with peoples and nations of the world to whom they were hitherto denied access.

The rapid pace of the tremendous events that are reshaping Africa into a wholly new continent and catapulting it into world-relatedness cannot be considered

apart from the dynamic changes of world social, economic, and political order as a whole. The rapidity of
the means of communication and transportation is bring-
ing the peoples and nations of the earth into closer
relationships. Moreover, the fact that the African continent is the last great repository of mineral resources, so
greatly in demand by the technological developments of
today's world, cannot help but thrust Africa and its new
nations into the vortex of the world situation. This would
be so, even if there were not the cold war developments
which have led the West and the Soviets into an increased rivalry for the minds and souls of the people of
Africa and for the tremendous quantities of mineral resources in the bosom of Africa's soil.

The sum and substance of this new international impact is the rediscovery of Africa by Western nations and
a discovery of Africa on the part of all the other nations
of the world that had no ties with the continent. On the
other hand, it has meant a discovery of the world by
Africans. Twenty years ago, only a few thousand Africans
were permitted to leave the continent to study abroad in
colonial countries, and few could cross the boundaries
established by colonial governments within the continent.
Today, African students not only go to colleges in other
African nations, but they are enrolled in universities
from Jerusalem to Peking and from Hawaii to Moscow.
Furthermore, unofficial delegations of labor, political, and
cultural groups and organizations are constantly on the
move seeking aid and support, attending conferences,
and making friends. Even before Kenya becomes fully
independent, its leaders opened up the world to Kenya.
Brilliant, indefatigable Tom Mboya and Jomo Kenyatta
changed Kenya from a spot on the map to a place to be
reckoned with. Four members of the Legislative Council
toured the Middle East and Asia in the fall of 1961,
and while Jomo Kenyatta was still under restriction at

Máralal, leaders of many countries beat a path to his door.

On my first extended trip to Africa in 1954, Africans in all countries were astounded that I had crossed so many boundaries and talked with so many of the leaders of neighboring countries. Even at that time, men who knew very little about the world beyond the boundaries of either their own local tribal areas or the borders of their countries had become aware of Africa as a whole. In Kenya, they asked me about what was then known as the Gold Coast. In Dakar, they were concerned about the organization of labor unions in the Camerouns. In the Congo, they wanted to know about developments in Nigeria. In Liberia, they raised questions about the Rhodesias. In Ethiopia, they were not disinterested in Africa south of the Sahara, as I had been led to believe. But in all countries they spoke with great feeling and in the most hostile tones about South Africa, Angola, and Mozambique. When I discussed the Mau Mau emergency with a group of students at the University College in Accra and referred to the terrorists' activities, one lad stood up to chastise me by saying, "Dr. Robinson, they are not terrorists, they are like your patriots in 1776 fighting for their land, their freedom, and for independence."

II

The rejection of colonialism has not and cannot move with the same speed in all countries. The speed depends upon a number of complex and interrelated factors that are different in different areas and under different colonial powers. It proceeded fastest and best where the controlling power was willing to recognize the changing facts of history and graciously prepared their people at home and the people of Africa for that change. It does not matter that this was done with some reluctance; the fact remains that it was done on occasion where there were no settlers, where there were no great industrial installations or discoveries of deposits of mineral wealth, and where there was a fairly sizable body of educated people. In these areas of West Africa the leaders and their people soon learned that violence was not the best or the only weapon of liberation. This is to a great extent also true in the culturally homogeneous areas of North Africa.

Contrariwise, it has proceeded more slowly in those areas where the colonial powers have not pursued an enlightened policy; where there has been unyielding resistance supported by a die-hard policy in Europe and encouragement from sympathizers in the United States and an intractable settler population in the African country. In countries like South Africa, Angola, Mozambique, and the Federation of Rhodesia and Nyasaland, Africans will ultimately, though in different degrees, reject colonialism and seek independence and an equal voice in government with whatever means are available to them. They have, nevertheless, shown that they prefer to achieve their ends with nonviolent methods.

A sad case in point is the turbulent and unhappy Congo—a land of great mineral deposits—where the ruling powers made no preparation for growth and change, discouraged higher learning to the extent of having only fourteen Africans of university graduate level out of 13,500,000 people, and perpetrated other equally negative policies dominated by an interest wholly committed to economic exploitation and a paternalism unequaled in colonialism.

One contemplates in horror the violence in the Congo indicative of the fate that might overtake those other areas which refuse to yield to history, time, and change. Though violence as a method of change is bestial and cannot be condoned, it is well to put these events in Africa in the framework of revolutionary changes in Europe's past which were accompanied by bloody strife. By comparison with Europe, the African situation up to now is a quiescent affair. It gives, fortunately enough, little evidence that it will be nearly as long as the European struggle for civil rights. Nonetheless, Africans will be satisfied with nothing short of the complete and final demise of colonialism.

The greatest single change is wrought by the breaking of the colonial ties that Africans have been hammering at for a long time. While rejecting colonialism and demanding the opportunity for self-government and independence, Africans have not wholly, out of hand, rejected Europeans, especially where Europeans have demonstrated a desire to share with them as equals and partners. It is, however, true that there is a long history of insolence and mistreatment of Africans by Europeans that has yet to be lived down. Stubborn resistance to African demands for treatment as equal members of the family of nations and of the human race and adherence to stringent racial segregation and the denial of basic opportunities under the formula of apartheid still bode ill for the future. However, in the main, Africans are still ready to work with people from Europe and America on the basis of mutual respect and equality. It simply remains for the former European colonial powers and their representatives to reciprocate on this common ground of mutual respect and partnership that Africans are seeking. Many Africans are not only aware of, but will readily concede to, the importance of the developments during the colonial epoch, even though the framework in which these developments were made is to them an anathema. They know, however, that whatever economic development and achievements were made in Africa were basically those of exploitation of both their people and their resources, in which they did not share to any considerable degree. They are simply not willing to have this situation continue, even if it would greatly improve their lot economically and socially.

President Sékou Touré, of Guinea, spoke for all Africans when he said, "We prefer independence and poverty to riches and slavery." Africans are just as willing to admit their agreement with, and appreciation of, the new aid programs of some of the European countries and the United States in their lands so long as this is not a neo-colonialism or a continuation of the old paternalism. In other words, they want political colonialism eradicated, but they will just as rigorously reject an economic colonialism.

The rejection of colonialism has finally begun to free African people and countries from the ties that bound them solely to European colonial powers and denied them access to the rest of the world. Until the last two or three decades, many of the African peoples had absolutely no contact with the rest of the world. It is equally important to understand that peoples of the various African nations had only minimal, if any contact at all, even with their neighbors. Members of tribal groups were isolated from one another by the arbitrary lines that often split the geographical areas where tribal and ethnic groups of the same family spread over a wide territory. Even though they were the same people and sometimes of the same family, they could not readily cross the arbitrary boundaries of the political divisions drawn by the Europeans.

But with the demise of colonialism, Africans have begun to discover Africa and the rest of the world, and the rest of the world has begun to discover them. Colonial disengagement of European powers has, therefore, created a desire on the part of Africans for engagement, not only with their near neighbors and peoples in even the remotest parts of Africa, but engagement with the other nations of the world, who were denied access to the continent and with whom Africans were neither permitted nor encouraged to develop relationships. Their recent discovery of one another and their developing relationships with nations around the world will move much more rapidly. The most important aspect stimulating this desire for mutual engagement is their common opposition to colonialism, their common desire to achieve independent status, equality, and respect from the other members of the family of nations, and their common need of all kinds of assistance and trade.

Interest in, concern for, and the resulting confrontation with Africans of other nations has been loosely but inaccurately referred to as Pan-Africanism. Pan-Africanism is destined to become a powerful force of change and will stimulate many more changes.

III

The new but always latent desire to understand and relate to the rest of Africa, beyond the boundaries by which they were formerly limited, has now become a reality. Not only do the new leaders among African students relate to Africans in the great university centers of other countries and get to know them, but Africans are traveling all over Africa in many different capacities, not the least of which are in response to the many efforts of Pan-Africanism, or the more specific and special conferences called by the churches, the labor unions, the Governments, and other organizations.

The new Pan-Africanism projected on the continent, usually regarded by Westerners as basically a political concept, is in reality much broader than the limited area to which most of us have assigned it. It is, in fact, a rallying cry for those with many motives but with a basic desire for something specific, authentic, and distinctive as they seek to shape a new African personality that is made possible today by a multitude of bewildering social, educational, religious, and political shocks that the people are sustaining. Pan-Africanism is a result of perhaps the most significant and greatest change in Africa—a change in attitude of people toward themselves as having equal worth and unique characteristics and contributions.

Poised as they are between the old civilization of Africa and the new civilization of the Western world, Africans are not the people they were three decades ago, nor have they been nor do they desire to be molded into the pattern of the peoples who are vying to imprint their own civilization upon African culture. While they desire to move out of the past, they do not on the other hand desire to be European, American, Russian, Asian, or anything else but what they themselves hope to become—a fact undoubtedly not fully recognized by those who seek to influence or to "win" Africans. Although they desire independence, freedom, education, and the progress of the modern world, they want more than anything else to be themselves.

This new recognition of the importance of self as they reach toward a new sense of self-respect and independence is an important fact with which most of us outside Africa must come fully to terms. Having begun to develop a new consciousness of personal pride and personal worth, Africans are done forever with paternalism, arrogance, and condescension, no matter from which ideology or area of the earth it comes. They have absolutely no complex about race or color. On the contrary, they are proud of their color, and they measure the worth and acceptability of many other people partly by it. No longer is a European or a person with a white skin thought to be better, more intelligent, or more important than an African, an Asian, or a Middle Easterner. In fact, whiteness of skin carries definite liabilities, even for many sincere and devoted missionaries. This does not mean that Africans fail to recognize the contribution of white men to Africa—far from it. Africans appreciate this contribution, and they also desire that those of every race, including the white race, who will believe in them and work with them as partners and equals, not only remain but come and join with them as they march toward new horizons in self-government and international relationships.

As it changes with dramatic speed a whole new continent is entering the main stream of its peoples' quest for human dignity. It is inevitable that the problem of "Who am I?" and "Where am I going?" should loom as large though not so overtly or articulately as material and political organizations in Africa's concept of its future. In the beginning the discredit of old African cultures and ways of life brought by the impact of Western civilization induced a number of Africans to reject the customs, rites, and rituals by which their fathers had achieved a sense of balance, dignity, and a satisfying relationship between the spiritual and material world. Today, however, after the first impression of this cultural and technological onslaught has worn off, more and more Africans are seeking a reinterpretation and a new pride in their old indigenous cultures without, at the same time, being immobilized by looking back too fondly and unobjectively upon former ancient grandeur. It is most unfortunate that most people in the West knew little of Africa's past, so willfully was it neglected by the Western conquerors and despoiled by the penetration of business and commerce. Indeed it was too little known and understood by Africans themselves. Nevertheless, Africa does have a substantial cultural heritage. Achieving a proper balance between the old and the new, will, in large measure, determine the continuation of African stability and progress in the future.

The psychological problems created by the necessary synthesis between old and new has important implications both for the Africans and for the people of other nations who must work out new relationships with them. To a greater extent than most Westerners believe, they must learn how to look at Africa through African eyes and minds. It is not only imperative for Africans undergoing great personal changes to apply their new knowledge and insights to gain a better understanding of themselves, it is also imperative for other peoples to utilize this knowledge for better insight and understanding of Africans and of themselves in relation to the Africans. In order to understand what is loosely referred to as African neutralism—very perplexing and frustrating to those who view African development naïvely and which will be dealt with more thoroughly in another chapter— it will be necessary to give more attention to this particular problem than we have heretofore, because it creates serious psychological problems for us as well as for the Africans. Otherwise, we will be led into a dead-end pursuit of illusions.

Perhaps the rapid pace of change and development in Africa can be fairly accurately gauged by a recital of a few startling facts:

1. Forty million Africans, more than a fifth of the total population, have moved from primitive villages of the rural areas to the modern cities within the last two decades. Perhaps 40 per cent of that number, overwhelmingly men, are constantly on the move from their villages to mines, industrial centers, commercial enterprises, and the great ports that have resulted from the discovery and development of and reliance upon the mineral resources in Africa by the Western world. A large number of single men are constantly moving between their home villages and the centers of their work where they stay for brief periods and return again while others

take their places. Consequently, the old tribal patterns of control are breaking down. Family structure is seriously disrupted and juvenile delinquency, a phenomenon unknown in the African tribal society, has reached serious proportions in all the large cities. These are obviously, of course, problems of urbanization that will continue as long as Africa develops and forges ahead in the development of its economic, political, and social structure.

2. American capital investments in Africa have increased since 1945 by nearly 3,000 per cent, and this is only the beginning. The storied resources of the continent will demand even larger investments in the future to meet the world needs that will be greatly increased by African demands for both capital and consumer goods as their economy moves forward and expands. Even a superficial accounting of the long list of vital and strategic minerals necessary to Western economy that comes out of Africa is enough to explain the continent's new importance, the rapid growth of its commerce and industry, and the development of its labor supply. But Africa's manpower and human resources—once educated, trained, and organized—are even more important than its mineral wealth.

3. Most Africans are workers. Therefore, labor unions that were just beginning a quarter of a century ago are today powerful and significant in all areas of free Africa. They are of increasing importance even in colonial areas where settlers have control of political and police power. These unions, formed and influenced by the World Federation of Trade Unions, such as the Confédération Générale du Travail in French-speaking areas, a largely leftist and sometimes communist-dominated movement, or by the International Confederation of Free Trade Unions, organized along more democratic lines, are bound to play an even more important role in Africa's future development. Whereas a quarter of a century ago less than 5,000

Africans belonged to labor unions, there are today over 1,700 locals.

4. Africans are more and more becoming aware of the wealth that lies in their soil. They know of the growing dependence of the Western world, particularly of the Soviets and the United States, on their mineral resources. They are also acutely aware of the fact that this dependence gives them an increased leverage both within the context of the cold war and outside of it.

5. Africans know that colonialism is either dead or dying and that the sooner it dies the healthier will be the world situation, including their own. While decolonization moves faster in some areas than in others, colonialism is doomed by the winds of change in every area of Africa. The African people know that they themselves will make decisions in all the areas of Africa. Despite the resistance and delaying tactics of such nations as Portugal and the Federation of the Rhodesias and Nyasaland and South Africa (the latter in a somewhat different category) Africans know that the hegemony of Europeans over the Africans in these areas is also doomed and that sooner than later new relationships will have to be worked out in which Africans are either partners or the dominant political force in those countries. The slogan of President Sékou Touré, of Guinea, "We prefer independence and poverty to riches in slavery," is deep within the heart and mind of every African in every part of Africa.

6. Twenty-five years ago, there were less than five hundred African students studying in European and American universities. Today, there are almost six times that many in the United States alone, ten times that many in the British Isles, at least eight times that many on the continent of Europe, including the Eastern-bloc countries, and at least as many, if not more, in the Middle East and Asia. This new and potential leadership will undoubtedly have a profound effect upon speeding up

even more rapidly the miraculous changes taking place. Furthermore, it will also bring an increased cross-fertilization of ideas.

7. The material changes each year not only in the cities but increasingly in the rural areas are stupendous, to say the least. One who travels to Africa every year is greatly impressed by the amazing increase in economic, social, industrial, political, urban, and transportation developments over the year before.

The rapid social changes and economic development in Africa are inevitable. Moreover, they will accelerate in rapidity as time moves on. Neither Africans, nor we ourselves, can hope for or wait for a more leisurely change in these developments. Basic changes in the world will not wait for the readiness of people. This will be as true in Africa as it has ever been in the past in every other nation in the world. To take refuge in the shibboleth that Africans are not ready is sheer folly. To shape a policy on the basis of unreadiness is not only to beg the main point, it is an indulgence in a dangerous fallacy of self-deception. No people are ever fully ready for progress and self-government. When the time comes, they either move with it or time leaves them behind. While some Americans drag their feet, arguing about readiness, others say join us, and we will help you to achieve your ambitions. A careful perusal of the early days of American history could prompt the same insidious question concerning the readiness of America in 1776 for the most dynamic revolution in human history. The leaders of the American Revolution simply took the tide of history at its flood to lead the nation on to fame and fortune. What we have done, others, including Africans, can surely do also.

Chapter III

Forces Changing Africa Today

AMONG THE MANY FORCES AT WORK IN CHANGING
Africa are religion, nationalism, communism, technological development, and the cross-fertilization resulting
from its new world-relatedness. These forces are catalytic
in that they continually generate new and correlative
forces that accelerate development, progress, and change.

I

As we look over the past, it is easily discernible that
the religious forces in Africa itself have been among the
most significant in helping to midwife the changes taking
place on that continent. No force was more powerful,
maintained a greater hold on the people, dominated their
culture, determined their social and family relationships,
and forged their economic and political concepts than the
old animistic religions. Although their day is rapidly passing, it would be inaccurate to say that there is not some
saving residue in Africa's ancient religions that helps to
provide an important bond with the past and a healthy
balance for the future of new Africa. Even in what some
supposedly more enlightened Westerners would call their
lowest state, the animistic religions of Africa provided a
sense of physical as well as psychological security.

When these beliefs were discredited or destroyed by

the penetration of the Christian missionary movement and to a larger extent in North Africa by the impact of Islamism, the resulting confusion created a great number of emotional and psychological shocks that the leaders of the penetrating religions never fully appreciated and which the Africans have only recently begun to understand and not yet to deal with realistically. These problems take on greater dimensions when it is realized that the colonial and political framework within which European and American missions had to operate denied Africans full access to the Western religious, political, and social institutions where they might have more quickly found a new sense of belonging.

Despite the confusion brought by the new religions, which helped to cast off the anchors of old traditions, both the Christian and the Moslem penetrations of the African continent may have been among the most powerful forces in reshaping its future and determining its progress. However, the latter of these two religious forces has not done so to the same degree. In some instances it has been a deterrent to modern African progress. While the hold of the animistic religions on the people of Africa has become tenuous, both the essence and the impact of Christianity and Islam not only created a new awakening but also opened up new horizons and inspired the people who embraced them to march into a new future.

Islam has gained twice as many converts as the Christian missionary forces, despite the fact that it started in North Africa with a three-hundred-year handicap. After the high-water mark of the early Christian movements in the second and third centuries, it had a powerful impact upon Africa in three major areas:

1. It provided, although not with overwhelming success, a means of unity as it swept away many of the animistic religions and bound the people together in a common religious framework and by the ninth century

established great empires even on the southern fringes of the Sahara. This provided, at least in part, a framework of brotherhood in which all believers were bound together, despite color, tribal groupings, political divisions, or cultural differences. Despite Islam's lack of social concern and educational and charitable organizations to meet basic social and economic needs, one nevertheless wishes that Christianity could have done as well in the areas of brotherhood as Islam.

2. Once it moved across the desert and south, Islam provided a bridge, however small, between the people of North Africa and those of Africa south of the Sahara. Furthermore, as far as it could go under the limited circumstances placed upon it by colonial powers, it provided a bridge toward the Middle East and Asia, which Africans prior to this time had never experienced. One remarkable aspect of Moslem penetration south of the Sahara is the fact that it had been achieved without a highly organized and centrally directed leadership.

3. Whatever the limitations of Islam from a Christian perspective, it nevertheless provided a powerful stimulus toward independence and self-determination, which is the greatest single hunger and desire in Africa. Because Islam was indigenous and was led by people of similar color, Islamic leaders could agitate for political reform with fewer handicaps than Christian missionaries who came from outside and had to operate within the framework of the colonial powers. It is of no little importance that these powers determined the policies by which Christian missionaries could be admitted into the areas they controlled. The religion of Islam was under no such disadvantage.

Notwithstanding the favorable position of Islam, it was the tremendous contribution of the Christian missionary movement that laid a solid and significant groundwork for the present developments in Africa despite the errors of many of the missionaries who laid that foundation. It simply cannot be denied that the change in attitudes toward self-respect and self-value, as Africans sought to find a new personality, was inspired and heightened by the Christian missions. Christianity not only helped the Africans to see themselves as creatures of equal worth in the sight of God but it lifted their horizon beyond the Middle East, the cradle of Christianity, and beyond the countries from which the missionaries came, to the whole world. This could happen even though colonial officials and leaders of the commercial enterprises opening up Africa's resources denied the full promise of the gospel they preached when it came to actual practice.

Almost equal in importance was the fact that the Christian missionary movement, more than any other single force in Africa, until recently provided the largest opportunity for education and the training of future leaders. It would be impossible to make a list of the present-day leaders of Africa without finding that perhaps three fourths of them, in one way or another, received their first educational experience in institutions provided by Christian missionary movements. The additional fact that thousands of Africans, below the top level of leadership, were educated and trained in these schools, is even more significant, because successful leadership demands enlightened followers on every level. Hence, the Christian educational work, even though it could not achieve anything approaching a mass basis until Africans began to get control of their own destinies, helped Africans to an enlightened and intelligent awareness of the world in which they live, to an understanding of how to deal with their problems, and provided the means by which they could develop the methods of applying the new knowledge to break the economic, political, social, cultural, and even the religious boundaries by which they were circumscribed. In essence this was a recognition of latent human dignity and the stimulation of the inspiration to explore the divine importance of both personal and national potentialities. As more indigenous African churches come under African influence, the rapid change in Africa, resulting from the impact of these forces, will accelerate.

II

However, the most powerful and important force in Africa today is nationalism, which is just at its beginning. Perhaps more than all other forces combined, nationalism has awakened in the African a sense of pride and self-respect, a sense of destiny and obligation, and an irrepressible desire to throw off the yoke of outside control. Although it is not yet in full bloom, it is sweeping the entire continent in one form or another.

This is not a nationalism of Europe or America or even Asia. Nothing so complex as nationalism can be transplanted from one continent to another without going through great and powerful changes. Undoubtedly the nationalism of Africa has been inspired by the West, by the hundreds of students who have gone abroad from the continent, by returning African soldiers at the end of World War II, by the relationship with colonial powers, and to a great extent by the missionary movement. Nevertheless, it has probably received its most recent and greatest encouragement from the success of the nationalistic movements, which brought the nations of Asia into new world-relatedness. It must, therefore, of necessity have different overtones, take on African characteristics, and reflect the multiplicity of its origins. But among all the sources of inspiration, Western nationalism will be dominant because of Africa's long association with the West. Beginning humbly, facing tremendous public pressure with very little funds but with dogged determination,

African leaders organized their followers and maintained their leadership even when colonial officials jailed them. The leaders could be incarcerated but the growing multitude of their followers increased with every act of colonial opposition and suppression. Ideas cannot be contained by prison walls nor hopes crushed forever by police action.

It was the organization and the backing of African political parties that gave their people a voice with which to state their case before the world. African political movements gained a power that could not be denied, and their leaders found the levers by which they could pry freedom from the hands of those who denied it to them. Not one of the outstanding political leaders of Africa who has come to power and has led his country to independence could have achieved these successes without the party that backed him.

The Congress Peoples Party in Ghana, the National Council of Nigeria and the Camerouns, the Action Party and the Northern Peoples Party in Nigeria, the Tanganyika African National Party in Tanganyika, the Sierra Leone Peoples Party in Sierra Leone, the Rassemblement Democratique Africain in the Ivory Coast, the Union Progressiste Senegolaise in Senegal, the Comité de l'Unité Togolaise in Togo, the Union pour la Communauté Franco-Africaine in Niger, and the Parti Sociale Democrate in Malagasy—these were the political parties and organizations which provided the strength and backing through which African leaders won independence. So long as the leaders could not be isolated their people's hopes would inevitably be realized.

In those countries not yet free, parties like the Movimento Popular de Liberatacao de Angola and Uniao dos Populacoes de Angola in Angola, the Malawi Congress Party in Nyasaland, the Union National Independence Party in Northern Rhodesia, the National Democratic

Party in Southern Rhodesia, the Kenya African National Union, and the Kenya African Democratic Union in Kenya will provide their leaders with the machinery, the support, and the power to usher in the freedom they seek. Furthermore, all of these parties provide the basis of responsible democratic government. Nonetheless, all of them, even in those countries that have attained their cherished goal, face many unsolved problems, challenges, and often opposition. In many cases both the parties and their leaders still have to learn first to tolerate, then understand and encourage responsible and healthy opposition. In many cases their reluctance, for the present, is derived from their newness to power, their fear of the opposition becoming a tool of forces they have so recently defeated. Whereas this rightly gives true believers in democracy cause for concern, in most cases it does not justify alarm. The growing process will take care of some of this intolerance, and the rising generation will take care of the rest of it.

Nationalism is the insatiable urge of people to achieve freedom, self-respect, self-government, and self-improvement. To accept nationalism is to accept the fact of life that every nation should have an equal opportunity to build a secure, peaceful world and that all men should and must be accepted as ends to the glory of God and the achievement of a more secure society and an interdependent international structure. In the past, Africans have learned from us and the people of Europe, and more recently from Asia, that no greater disaster can come to a people than to lose their sovereignty to the domination of outsiders. On the other hand, they know that a nation cannot make progress without self-government and the right to participate as equals in the family of nations. They have seen from firsthand experience what national unity, self-respect, individual initiative, self-government, and an enlightened, educated people can produce in the way of personal as well as national progress, development, and security.

The political parties of Africa—the practical way in which nationalism organizes and expresses itself—are becoming more fully developed and better led in every part of Africa. All over the continent today one finds every kind of youth, women, civic, and national movements with political potential in various stages of development. These movements command a participation and allegiance such as no colonial government could ever obtain. For the exploiter can neither understand nor touch the soul of the exploited, although he may shackle the spirit temporarily. The loyalty of Africans to their political parties and leaders is the envy of the most devout missionary.

Kenneth Kaunda of Northern Rhodesia and Dr. Hastings Banda of Nyasaland are far more important in African thinking than Prime Minister Macmillan of England. Sékou Touré of Guinea and President Senghor of Senegal have a wider and more lasting appreciation in the hearts and minds of Africans than General DeGaulle. Premier Balewa and Governor General Azikiwe of Nigeria and President Nkrumah of Ghana have a more powerful impact upon African thinking than President Kennedy or his famous predecessor President Franklin D. Roosevelt. One can say the same of Julius Nyerere, of Tanganyika, Jomo Kenyatta and Tom Mboya, of Kenya, and President William V. S. Tubman, of Liberia. These men speak with an authority and influence in parts of Africa beyond their own borders that Premier Khrushchev, of Russia, can never hope to achieve. It was a strange twist, although not an unusual fact of history, that even while Kenyetta was in prison he was the single most powerful man in Kenya, the British Governor General and the white settlers not excepted.

On the other hand, no European or American leader enjoys so high a place in the hearts and minds of Africans as Prime Minister Nehru. When it is considered that Mr. Nehru has few resources from which to give foreign aid, his stature with Africans assumes an even larger and more powerful role. Reflection upon this fact should have a sobering effect upon our thinking.

Not only do African nationalist groups and political organizations agitate for independence at home, they also raised money before most of their countries were free to send representatives to the capitals of Europe, Asia, and the United States and to the United Nations to plead their cause. Moreover, they have set up leadership training schools and raised funds quite on their own to send some of their brightest students to the great university centers of the world. They have not limited their efforts to the organization of rallies, boycotts, and strikes but initiated projects for social improvement and self-help.

The bill of particulars and the current of ideas of nationalism sweeping through Africa are not unlike those articulated by the patriots of our country prior to the war which secured American independence. The masses of Africa at the village level may not yet be able to verbalize their basic hopes and aspirations, but they know clearly what they want. Above all, they have a small but able and skillful leadership and a larger reservoir of rising, eager, impatient young people of great potential ability. They are inspired—and it is well for us to remember this—by the same ideals that inspired the bold initiators of democratic institutions and government in our country, in France, and in England. They are not greatly impressed by our military power, and they despise the explosion of nuclear weapons. However, they are desirous of working with us and not against us, although they are somewhat suspicious of our motives and are not sure that economic and financial power will not result in the same exploitation as European military power. More than anything else they want world partnership, for they are forever done with the stepchild role that their fathers were forced to play. They would like to be loved, but they would rather be respected.

The nationalism of Africa is an altogether good, wholesome, and positive force. However, there are two great dangers inherent in it and one great danger lurking outside it. First, the desire to get things done quickly by over-all planning, without sufficient educational and technical preparation and a secure economic foundation, can lead to strong totalitarian control. Nonetheless, it is only natural when viewed from past historical, political, and cultural development that African governments will be led by strong individual personalities, and this should not unduly disturb us. Second, dismal failure in the attempt to achieve desired ends too quickly will precipitate a disillusionment of the masses to such an extent that the resulting vacuum will be filled with an explosive rebellion as easily vented against the most likely scapegoats, the Western powers, as against leaders within the country. The ever-present danger waiting patiently outside is communism, which seeks to identify itself with national aims and aspirations and make capital out of failure.

It will be to the great advantage of every nation in the world, and to the West in particular, to do more than supply a pittance of technical experts, disseminate a little technical knowhow, and start a few agricultural, industrial, educational, and electrical projects. It must be paramount in our thinking that whatever we do, although motivated by both altruistic motives and enlightened self-interest, in the final analysis it must be for the major benefit of Africans and in no sense an effort to superimpose our institutions upon Africa. Our efforts must be adequate if we attempt them at all, and our planning must be long range and comprehensive of the total problem in conjunction with Africans, who must have an equal right to say what that planning will be. Such a

plan presupposes a self-discipline and a sharing of resources as we have not yet envisioned. It also presupposes
the necessity for significant changes in the attitude of
outside nations toward the people of Africa, which must
precede the creation of an adequate international, political
formula.

III

The impact and influence of communism on the changes
taking place in Africa are not clearly defined but they
are nevertheless very real. No one knows the extent of
the communist movement in Africa with any certainty,
but it has raised its troublesome head in a great many
places. Its growth and spread in Africa is difficult to determine for several reasons:

1. It is not the nature of communism to advertise its
tactics of infiltration or its next steps. It deliberately
seeks to confuse issues in order to keep its strategy in
doubt.

2. Communism comes to Africa, as indeed it goes to
all underdeveloped areas of the world, in many guises,
making common cause with legitimate grievances and
aspirations.

3. It has been all too easy to confuse African tribal
collectivism, which in itself is not communism, with the
Marxian dialectic.

Communism accommodates its tactics to the situation
in which it operates but in the last analysis it has only one
ultimate end in view—to subvert or destroy what is inimical to itself and then take control. Its influence upon
the developments in Africa, though more indirect than
direct, must be viewed with seriousness but not with
alarm. Otherwise, we will develop a fearful, negative and
oversimplified strategy that will do more harm to our relationships with Africans and actually help communism

toward its goals by playing into some predetermined role.

It goes without saying that undoubtedly there have been some Africans who honestly believe that as long as communism frightens Europeans and Americans, they can utilize it to their own ends and reject it when it no longer suits their advantage or ultimate purposes. There are other Africans who believe that only the communist leaders want really to help them to full freedom and self-government. The greatest aid to communist infiltration and penetration in Africa is not so much to be attributed to the susceptibility of Africans as it is related to failures on the part of the West to give the fullest possible aid to African aspirations for freedom and independence.

The misuse of the communist issue on the part of Western nations—branding socialists and other nationalistic leaders in Africa as communists or fellow travelers— is highly irresponsible and plays into the hands of communist strategists. What some Africans consider a Western obsession with "the communist danger" has tended to discredit both the sincerity and the real basis of the Western concern over communists' intentions. African leaders feel more and more that Western emphasis upon the dangers of communism in Africa is in essence condescension to African ability and leadership. Nevertheless the danger of communist influence is greatest during the early and more impressionable periods of African development and change, when Africans may be so preoccupied with the shedding of an old colonialism as to be unmindful of the dangers that the new colonialism of communists may present.

Although the encroachment of communism is spotty and sometimes exaggerated, it is nevertheless very real. Diplomatic activity by Soviet Russia, the Eastern European, and Chinese Governments has greatly increased in Africa. The establishment of embassies and consulates has been accompanied by trade, industrial, and cultural missions from the Soviet Union, the satellite countries, and China. As a result there has been a great deal of increased travel and exchange between the capitals of communist-bloc countries and many of the new nations of Africa.

Perhaps the major communist effort is geared not so much toward political penetration as it is toward winning the minds and souls and influencing the thinking of the rising generation of future leaders. The apparatus to infect and influence the minds of young Africans both at home and wherever they are studying abroad is heavily financed, whether these students are in communist or in noncommunist countries.

Soviet tactics are very clever in their ability to hold firmly to the desired end and at the same time make shifts and changes as convenience dictates. The Russians have a remarkable facility to change the means by which the end is to be gained. In the early fifties communist strategy was built around the united-front technique, but about 1955 this tactic was changed to one of concentration upon strengthening the local communist elements in the various areas. It was decided to minimize alliances with organizations and groups that were recognized as noncommunist and therefore as forces that had to be reckoned with and, if possible, neutralized by flattery. The necessity for this change in strategy was brought home to the communists by the effectiveness of the noncommunist nationals who gathered in April, 1955, at the Asian-African Conference in Bandung. Rebuffed in this conference, communists sought to gain entrance to Africa through the back door. To achieve this end they became very active in organizing the Afro-Asian Peoples' Solidarity Conference in Cairo in December, 1957. However, the advantage was short lived. By the end of 1960, at the second Afro-Asian Peoples' Solidarity Conference at Conakry, Guinea, an effort, similar to the one made at Cairo in 1957–1958 and later at the All African Peoples' Convention, to block the creation of a separate Pan-African organization, which communists could not effectively control, met a severe setback. In the subsequent All-African Peoples' Conferences and the Afro-Asian Youth Conference of February, 1959, the communists were thoroughly unmasked as perpetrators of a new colonialism and came under their heaviest attack and criticism. This led to their exclusion from the plenary sessions scheduled for 1960.

However, one should not take too much comfort in the fact that communism was defeated on these occasions. These must be considered as only temporary setbacks, for there is no missionary in the world so tenacious, unyielding, and patient as the communist missionary. He thoroughly believes that importunity ultimately wins its consent against the most reluctant.

In the final analysis the Africans can deal more successfully with communism in their continent than anyone else. As Nigeria—which after only one and a half years of independence feels politically mature enough to allow the distribution of communist literature—is demonstrating, Africans are not likely to exchange white masters for red masters, or economic exploiters for ideological exploiters.

Although some few Africans seem to have been infatuated with the appeal of communism, they were seeking material aid and assistance while making up their own minds about accepting proffered ideologies. Sometimes they were driven to the necessity of turning eastward by the mistakes and ineptness of Western powers—our own country included. That many African countries did not move farther into the Soviet orbit is more to the credit of the Africans than it is to any action on our part.

The evidence from history is both revealing and salutary. Ethiopia has long had communist aid but hasn't gone communist. Guinea accepted Soviet aid after we—

fearful of incurring French displeasure—also turned our backs on them in their hour of greatest material need of assistance. But Guinea is becoming increasingly wary. Liberia, though long courted by the Soviets, never succumbed. Even the troubled and buffeted Congo, within two months of a great tidal wave of Soviets, forced them out of the country with no help or assistance from us. And more recently, Guinea has had its share of disillusionment to the point of requesting the Soviet ambassador's recall.

Africans have and are learning that communists put a high price on their aid. Their supposed friendship and support of underdeveloped peoples is calculated to put into effect what Majhemout Diop, the African communist theoretician has proudly announced: "Communists put conditions on aid that they give to national democratic movements, if these movements are bourgeois. . . . International Communism must conclude temporary alliances with the democratic bourgeoisie in colonies and backward countries but must never fuse with them and must, without reservation, always defend the independence of the proletarian movement even when the latter is very embryonic."

Chapter IV

Rapid Changes Demand New Strategies

I

THE RAPID PASSAGE OF TIME, WHERE HISTORY IS foreshortened in the social, political, and economic developments of the African continent raises an urgent demand upon us to evolve bold, new relationships with changing Africa. The line from James Russell Lowell's poem, "Once to Every Man and Nation": "New occasions teach new duties, time makes ancient good uncouth," can be applied with peculiar relevance to the African situation in which we find ourselves involved.

The old policy of the United States, or lack of policy, was based on neutrality between African aspiration and European control. This policy simply will not suffice today. Our stubborn refusal to recognize the new sources of power in the African continent that have negated the importance of European colonial allies and our reluctance to develop concrete and creative relationships with the new nations could only make it difficult, if not altogether impossible, for us to share in the future of Africa. These attitudes could also lead us in the pursuit of illusions which could be dangerous to our survival. Fortunately, within the last five years there has been increasing evidence of the development of a more positive, imaginative, and direct relationship with the new African nations.

48

However, the emergence of that new attitude must proceed with much greater speed in the next half decade than it has in the past.

Before we can begin to determine the basis upon which we must develop the new strategy with Africa, we must frankly face our failures in the past. An honest evaluation will help us to clear our thinking in order to avoid pitfalls and to develop sound procedures for the future. Actually we will only be making clear to ourselves what the new African leaders have understood about us all along. But the most compelling reason for taking stock of our previous situation, as we try to evolve a new positive outlook, is that honest recognition of difficulties is a much-needed therapy before adequate changes and new approaches can be soundly developed.

In the first place, having carried out our policies toward Africa through European channels and in accordance with European dictates, we never found it necessary to develop anything like an adequate apparatus by which we could be related to the continent. Until only recently Africa was the way station for foreign service officers in their early years as they headed up the ladder or in their latter years before entering retirement. Until less than half a dozen years ago we had only a small, ill-organized, under-manned, and consequently ineffective section in our State Department to advise the Government about Africa—the world's second largest continent. The few clear voices in both the administration and the legislature went unheeded. This was largely because we were dependent upon European sources for both our information and to a large extent our guidance. In fact, it might well be said that our actions in and toward Africa were but an appendage to our European policy.

Tied as we were to our European allies, most of whom dominated the African continent in one area or another, we developed a tightrope balancing act between Europe and Africa when the new countries of that continent began to assert themselves and move rapidly toward independence. This second stage, though not worthy of us, was nevertheless better than the previous negative attitude of no policy whatever. It at least recognized the necessity for a change in our relationships since Africa's new importance in global affairs made it inevitable that we would be involved to a larger degree than ever before. It was, however, at this second stage that we established in 1956 a semiautonomous unit for African Affairs in the Department of State.

Whereas the former policy of negativism dissipated any capacity we might have had to fulfill a constructive function, the change, be it ever so little, was a recognition that the United States, if it is to lead a global coalition for freedom and independence, could not declare itself to be a nonparticipant in African affairs. It is undoubtedly true that the dramatic march of events in recent years not only in Africa but in the global struggle between the free and the controlled world helped to evolve this second step, out of which has grown a third step—the beginning of a creative and positive policy.

Although it is true, it is all too easy to take refuge in the excuse that our slowness was due to the lack of direct contact or association with Africa and the necessity of maintaining friendly relationships with our European allies. We were further deterred by political and military considerations and commitments that we felt we could not jeopardize. But beyond both of these factors was the even more powerful consideration of large American financial investments in Africa that helped to determine our actions in far more important ways than most Americans knew. In addition, it was hard, if not altogether impossible, for us to face the fact that since we had not developed basic repect for Negroes of African descent who had been citizens of our country for many generations, we would not find it easy to show any higher respect for Africans, who were thought of as backward, inferior peoples from the Dark Continent.

These, nevertheless, are but secondary contributing factors. The chief stumbling block was the fact that the United States could not, because of what it believed was enlightened self-interest, assert itself against the colonial attitudes and policies of its allies. Nevertheless, such opposition to African nationalism is a luxury that neither the European nations nor the United States can any longer afford. In a report prepared in 1959 for the Senate Foreign Relations Committee, Dr. Melvin Herskovitz of the African Studies Program at Northwestern University wrote: "The United States has never had a positive, dynamic policy for Africa. Until very recently we have looked to the continuing control of that continent by friendly European powers as a guarantee of stability and dependable co-operation and have been reluctant to acknowledge the principle of self-government as fully applicable to its people."

Fortunately, however, the third stage in our relationship has begun, namely, a reappraisal of our relationship to the African nations and a more positive position with our allies about the necessity of such reappraisal both on our part and on theirs. The development of this new attitude is recognition of the fact that we have seen enough of the rapid pace of emerging Africa to know that Africans desire that no nation or group of nations shall hold dominance over them; that the pace of events and the forces of nationalism can no longer be controlled by Europeans; that there is urgent necessity and wisdom in evolving our own direct relationships with independent nations of the continent; that we must hasten the speed of the demise of colonialism and offer every available constructive aid we can to the nations seeking help with their problems as they move into the family of nations; that if we do not proceed from these considerations, we are actually acting against our own best interests, as well as the best interests of our allies and the African countries.

The new policy has lifted us out of the dilemma where we sought to find a compromise between what we believed in terms of individual rights, freedom, and independence and the legitimate aspirations of African peoples, and what, on the other hand, we apparently believed to be the requisites of Western unity. This false strategy of lofty tributes to the principles of self-determination on one side, and the avoidance of actual support of this determination on the other, brought great confusion in the minds of the Africans. Many Africans and Asians sat in despair as they watched American statecraft squirm its way through Trusteeship Council meetings of the United Nations if indeed we did not altogether abstain when great issues of freedom and democracy were at stake.

The immorality of this position at the time can be clearly seen from the fact that the Trusteeship Council is the heir of the League of Nations' mandate system that first established the principle of international accountability for dependent areas. This, in turn, grew out of the idea that Woodrow Wilson fought for so hard in the old League of Nations and Secretary of State Cordell Hull enlarged and fostered with the enthusiastic support and endorsement of President Franklin Roosevelt. Thus we were denying the basic instrument we originally fostered, and we were doing this at a time when some of the most important world issues were being debated

Nevertheless, we have made a large step—our longest to date—in raising the African unit to a bureau status in the State Department, by greatly enlarging the staff, and opening many new consular offices. We have established new embassies, initiated a leadership grant program for

African leaders, and developed many new foreign aid programs and information service agencies in Africa. We now have a solid foundation on which to build for the future. We have come to see the reality of the possibility of developing a policy favorable toward Africa without alienating our allies. In more than one way, our new independence in thinking and action is a boon to our allies in Africa.

The number, capability, and quality of United States representatives in Africa are far superior in every respect to those who represented America only a few years ago. Their work is greatly aided by their sympathetic understanding of the emerging African nations and the new independent judgment and action of the nation they represent. This in turn is enhanced by the new appreciation for Africa and its leaders and a recognition of their strategic importance in world affairs. Perhaps the single, most important fact is that we are now dealing with African issues on their own merits.

A multitude of private organizations, taking their cue from a revolutionary United States policy, have rapidly risen to enlarge cultural, religious, educational, and economic ties between the United States and the new nations of Africa. The responsiveness of American citizens of all ages to the new opportunities opened up to both Africans and Americans is an encouraging awakening to the unlimited benefits that will accrue to both our peoples.

Major steps have been taken by reversing our former positions from abstention to positive, affirmative action, both within and without the United Nations, with regard to the problems posed by Angola, Southwest Africa, and South Africa. Thus one of the largest blots on the picture of traditional United States opposition to hindrances to self-determination and freedom was removed from our image in Africa. These actions speak more loudly than anything we can say.

Admittedly the task we face in Africa is not an easy one. Our new policy, no matter how fast, creatively, or constructively we develop it, will not find the going easy in overcoming African suspicion of both our motives and our strategy. We need to understand how difficult it will be to persuade Africans that we actively sympathize and will more actively work for the fulfillment of their aspirations. We need also to be patient with their skepticism that our interest now is mainly due to our involvement in the cold war and that we seek to involve them on our side. It is also true that Africa is fraught with many complex, internal problems, both between the new nations and their former colonial overlords, which are now compounded by the discovery of Africa by the rest of the world. Never before in history has the rest of the world had such a tremendous impact on one continent.

II

No matter how intricate, delicate, and touchy these problems are, they are not beyond human comprehension. If they are dealt with constructively, they are not insoluble. Americans have fallen too often and too long for the shibboleth that since we have not developed any historical relationships in these complex, underdeveloped areas, it is impossible for us to be as effective as the former colonizers who developed a great wealth of insight, personnel, and experience for the tasks they faced. The fact to remember is that while their insights might have been valid at one period in history, their experience and their relationships are no longer altogether valid for the new Africa. Nevertheless, it would be an optimistic fallacy, if not recklessness, to deny the magnitude of the difficulties of the decisions that now await us, as we seek to develop our new relationships with the African continent. But recognition of the enormity of the problems and the means to meet them is the first step toward the development of a whole new policy. Although many Africans are skeptical and suspicious of us because of our inherited past failures, only a few are hostile and most would like to believe in us and work with us on terms of equality and mutual respect.

One of the great emotional difficulties that Americans have had to overcome is the problem of resolving anxieties about how fast Africans can move into independent control of their own countries and the development of successful, sound, balanced international relationships with foreign countries. It is obviously impossible to look at Africa as a whole because of the great differences in development and levels of preparation. These differences are a result of the wide variances in the attitude of the colonial powers and the speed or lack of speed with which they have determined to help either to bring Africans to independence and self-government or to hold off the inevitable as long as possible. Africans are in a hurry—time will not stand still. The historical developments into which they have been swept for good or ill will hasten the prospect.

The time is never right for historical developments to mature. Honest and sincere men with vision, who are willing to accept the risks of the present, to live and work sacrificially and put their beliefs into practice, help to make the time right. This has been the encouraging experience of our own history as well as that of many other peoples. It will be no less true for Africans. But one of the great difficulties in America is the large number of our citizens who project the chaotic and confused situation in the Congo to the whole of Africa. They not only judge African progress from the vantage point of our total achievement since independence but also measure Africa's best by its worst.

While Africans are in a hurry, they themselves want

orderly, regular advancement as much as we do. The difference is that they have more confidence in being able to achieve this and more willingness to accept the risks involved in setting target dates that are not too far distant. Africans realize the possibility of unforeseen events as much as we do. But they are willing to take calculated risks with these events rather than to delay indefinitely the establishment of goals and target dates. Reluctance on our part to work with Africans in this step-by-step development, or even worse, by delaying tactics on our part because we believe they are attempting the impossible, shakes their confidence, arouses old suspicions, increases their frustrations, and at the same time strengthens the more violent elements that are always within any country, old or new.

But the question is persistently raised in the United States as to whether Africans are ready for independence and freedom. The question, whether or not it is an honest one, usually implies a large area of doubt in the thinking of most Americans. And because so many Americans have that doubt, they cannot bring themselves to develop a positive strategy to encourage and assist African advancement. Such feet-dragging vacillation is detrimental both to Africa's future and American prestige, but it will hurt America more than it will slow down the Africans' march to full freedom and independence.

However, a review of our own history would have been helpful to us in making a more adequate and constructive decision in this regard. Unfortunately, we usually judge underdeveloped nations from the perspective of our present development and achievement. This is obviously wrong and unfair. What needs to be done is to compare the present developments in Africa with the developments in our country as we moved toward independence and self-determination in the earlier days of our history. The question of whether or not we were ready was undoubtedly raised by many European countries and especially by the people of Great Britain from whom we were breaking away. From this perspective it can be seen quite easily that although there are many different educational, tribal, historical, and cultural problems with which the new Africa is beset, nevertheless in our early days we had many of the same agonizing problems of preparation and development.

If Africans believe that we believe in them and are willing to work with them, both directly and through the United Nations, for the achievement of an orderly, progressive march toward self-government and the building up of their nations, they will be more receptive to advice and guidance from us. Furthermore, it has been seen that the establishment of a reasonable timetable has had a remarkable psychological effect on the people of the country as well as on the leaders. It must not be forgotten, however, that the economic development must go hand in hand with orderly, political development toward self-government. No stability in Africa can ever be lasting unless this two-pronged attack is undertaken and vigorously prosecuted.

III

There is still another important area in which America has to make up its mind about its relationship with the developments in Africa that will encourage further confidence on the part of Africans in us and stimulate our development of helping programs. This is the perplexing problem of neutralism which is often confused in the United States with outright communism or a tendency toward communism. Failure to understand African neutralism and to relate to it in a positive way, will in a large measure determine how readily we can develop our own strategies in relationship to the countries of that continent.

To equate it naïvely with communism or communistic influence is both dangerous and detrimental.

Actually, African neutralism, as it is called, is rooted in the desire for international independence. Africans believe that it is for them and them alone to determine both their goals and their directions. They also believe that it is the responsibility of neither the West nor the East, the free world nor the communist world, to force their behavior patterns, values, institutions, and techniques upon them. What we need to understand is that African states are so new. They do not want to be swept up on either side of the cold war and thereby caught in the East-West power struggle. They feel, and rightly so, that if they throw their weight completely to either side, it will strengthen that side and may hasten the development of untoward events that can actually bring the world to the brink of the cataclysmic war it seeks to avoid.

Furthermore, African states are absorbed in their own internal problems. What we consider neutralism is simply an exhibition of their independence and self-pride. Here again a recollection of history might be helpful to American thinking, namely, the fact that in the early days of our own independence we zealously sought to avoid becoming entangled in foreign alliances.

It is very wrong to think that African neutralism is inimical to American goals and interests. Genuine African neutralism, and most of it is genuine, is not adverse to the United States nor to the interests of the United States. In fact, genuine neutrality can be a useful balance wheel in a world that is becoming more and more precariously balanced between two gigantic power factors.

At this stage of their history, Africans feel they must be free to seek help without ties and prior conditions of commitment to join an ideological bloc on either side. Wise handling of this reality, both in the aspect of its political nature and in the area of carefully conceived and thoughtfully developed cultural and aid programs, will greatly determine the success of our new engagement with the African nations.

If we persist in equating African neutralism with communism and communistic influence, no matter what policies we develop, how hard we work, or how much money we put into the support of aid programs we can but end in dismal failure. It is not an independent, though uncommitted Africa, which we have to fear, but a communist-dominated Africa. The latter would unquestionably be a great threat to the United States. But the prospect of communist domination is very remote, not because of any wisdom or particular aid program on our part. Africans are determined to defend their right to evolve the new African personality as indigenously African.

IV

The extraordinary change in strategy of the United States Government in its African policy has been matched by an even more extraordinary acceleration of interest and activity in Africa during the last decade on the part of many citizens groups, colleges, and voluntary agencies. These institutions have spread across the nation like wildfire to create excellent African programs. Some are secular, dealing in social welfare, cultural and technical programs; others are informational and educational. All are designed to further better African-American relationships, provide aid, and increase understanding by building bridges of friendship.

The impact of these groups has helped, even forced, the Christian missionary groups that pioneered in Africa since 1822 to revamp and improve their methods and emphases. The great contribution of Christian missions in social welfare, health, and education, despite the limitations under which the colonial powers allowed them admission to the areas, is not to be denied even by those who scoff at the religious penetration. Even the hard-bitten and cynical Stanley was moved, when he found David Livingstone, to write in his diary: "When I saw those enlightened sons of Africa whom he had brought to the faith, I also became a Christian standing by his side." Missions and the churches of America still have an important although a greatly different role within and under the African church. Only by rethinking this role will they be able to make progress and remain on the continent. The new challenges and opportunities for the churches and Christian missions in Africa will be dealt with in the last chapter of this book.

When I was a student at Lincoln University in the middle thirties, studying political science under Benjamin Azikiwe, the present Governor General of Nigeria, then a highly intelligent but lowly instructor from Nigeria pursuing part-time graduate courses at the University of Pennsylvania, there was only a handful of African students. These were chiefly in the Negro colleges of this country. There were hundreds of colleges with little interest in Africa and less interest in African students. Most of the African students arrived here almost penniless, with few friends, and against the wishes of the colonial administrators. They were often destitute, hungry, and ill-clothed for America's rigorous winters. They were a hearty lot and no amount of ridicule, privation, or prejudice could deter them from the pursuit of their goals. The church I pastored gave some support to many and, unfortunately, I buried not a few of them who died penniless and alone, during the first decade of my ministry.

At the time there were only a few organized groups of American citizens and foundations (New York Colonization Society, Friends of Liberia, Phelps Stokes Fund, Carnegie Foundation, Rockefeller Foundation) seeking to establish bridges of friendship between Liberia, the British areas, and the United States. The only exception was the Marcus Garvey Back to Africa Movement, which never really took root or captured the imagination of American Negroes to any considerable degree. No white people took interest in the back-to-Africa movement and only a few worked on the fringes of other agencies interested in Africa.

A few years later, a left-wing group known as the Council on African Affairs, with communist orientation and adhering to the party line, was organized in New York City. Even if we despise their reason for existence and their objectives, it should be said to their credit that they at least recognized the need to develop organization and strategy for the events taking shape in Africa. This was part of the strategy to influence Africans. It was also an effort, after miserable failure, insidiously to recapture the loyalty and support of American Negroes. A few bold voices among Negro historians, sociologists, and anthropologists, and a few far-seeing white people tried vainly to arouse the American conscience and awaken it to the new challenges and opportunities, but they were voices crying in the wilderness.

In the late forties, an imaginative Nigerian student, Kingsley O. Mbadiwe, succeeded in getting the support of a significant group of political, educational, business, and social leaders of both races to help organize the African Academy of Arts and Research. Unfortunately, after four or five years the organization was disbanded following Mr. Mbadiwe's return to Nigeria where he became Minister of Transportation and Communication and recently an advisor to Prime Minister Tawafa Balewa. The effort was not entirely lost because it served the useful purpose of calling attention to the advances in Africa, the shift of the centers of power and the aspirations of Africa. It represented the first effort to assist more African students to come to the United States for education and to help students in financial difficulty.

It is a favorite pastime of Americans to blame their Government and its leaders for failures in domestic and foreign policies. The truth is, however, that government in a democracy is a reflection of the basic attitudes, aspirations, and actions of its citizens. The failure of our Government referred to in a previous chapter is a failure of our people. A democratic government is no more than the will of its citizens. While it is the duty of officials to lead, they can go no faster and no farther than the people are willing. With no better attitudes than our nation possessed toward its millions of loyal citizens of African origin, it was not likely that we should have had a more enlightened attitude toward Africans, sad and deplorable as that fact may be.

Once the light began to dawn through the efforts of a few adventurous and enlightened spirits across this land, things began to change slowly. Better and more enlightened policies and actions were organized both at Government and at private levels. A large share of the credit for this maturing of attitudes is due to the increasing number of African students who began to spread out across the country as they sought education in our institutions. In pursuing their studies they became builders of friendship bridges. They increased our knowledge of Africa, awakened our interest, and challenged our conscience and our religious concern. Today there are over 2,500 African students of all classifications in this country, and more will come.

Second to the influence of the students in generating interest is the influence of our colleges and universities that were most generous in offering scholarship aid. The increase of African students is due to these factors to which must be added the change of power from European colonial officers to African hands. Perhaps the greatest opportunity we have is that African students increasingly seek opportunities in the United States, despite the unfortunate prejudices they must face, rather than accept greater financial assistance elsewhere, including the enticing offers of the Soviet Union.

But the problem is much too big to be continued on a disorganized, piecemeal basis, as the December 1961 conference at Racine, Wisconsin, outlined. The Racine conference received the report of the International Institute of Education on the "Survey of the African Student—His Achievements and His Problems." Fortunately, the urgency of this report and the necessity for implementing it by the organization and co-ordination of effort has been recognized by private and Governmental agencies attempting, with good promise, to work out an over-all plan. Training future leaders who return to take the reins of responsibility at home can be one of our best contributions to the African nations.

Real encouragement may be taken from developments among private and voluntary organizations on the American scene and from the great foundations that are taking a new and large interest in Africa. Among these are: the new African Studies Programs at the University of California at Los Angeles, Northwestern, Boston, Syracuse, Johns Hopkins, Columbia, Lincoln, and Howard Universities; the American Committee on Africa, Operation Crossroads Africa, the African-American Institute, the Experiment in International Living, the American Society for African Culture, African Studies Association, Africa Service Institute, African Research Foundation, American Universities Field Staff, Institute of International Education, International Friends of Ghana, Ruth Sloan Associates, Hazen Foundation, Ford Foundation, Foundation for all Africa, Carnegie Foundation for International Peace, and a number of others. There are at least a hundred well-organized agencies, and the list is added to almost every week. Many of the large United States business corporations with extensive interests on the continent are also formulating enlightened policies in Africa.

The full impact of the organizations in the United States developing plans and programs in Africa was felt and seen at the UNESCO Conference on African Affairs in Boston, Massachusetts (October, 1961), when over two thousand delegates gathered to exchange ideas, to evaluate their efforts, to regroup their forces, in planning for the immediate years ahead. Private organizations in many instances have gone ahead of the Government, and this is as it should be. The Government now lends every encouragement and facility, and then uses both the ideas and the personnel developed through these agencies to help shape its strategy and programs in Africa. Both Government and private agencies stimulate and reinforce each other to the benefit of both Africa and America.

Chapter V

The Responsibility of American Christians

THE CHURCH AND ITS MISSIONS ARE ALSO AT THE crossroads in Africa. Neither the church nor its missions exist in an immortal, holy vacuum but within the context of our human and sinful society. They do not stand apart from the world. In the light of the revolutionary crisis that has overtaken the missionary movement, we may well ask what are the churches to do? How are they to recover the motivation and the initiative for the redemption of Africa that led the early missionaries to venture into the spiritual and geographical jungles of that long-slumbering continent? What will be their role in the new African nations? How must they redeploy their resources, reorganize their tactics, and give life to plans that have been on paper for a long time? And above all, what adjustments can they make to the new centers of power and how must they relate to the new Governments?

The social and political upheavals under which Africa has been laboring leave no time for leisurely discussion and projection of plans but demand immediate action. Important decisions will have to be made, for the church, too, has a stake in Africa's future no less than it has had an important role in Africa's past. Our race for souls and the hearts of men on that continent is a race against time. I know only one way in which we can cleanse ourselves so that Christ may reconcile that part of the world through

65

us: to launch forth upon a bold and creative program of sufficient depth and co-ordination of all the religious forces. Africa can be the achievement of the Christian church of this century if we but proceed in the faith that God has called us to "lay hold with impatient hands" in that area of the world to prepare for the coming of his Kingdom. With colonialism passing into oblivion, we can no longer justify missionary efforts that do not take African Christians into full partnership of policy-making and administration. It is obligatory that we change as rapidly as possible from a missionary structure to a fraternal-worker emphasis. At the same time this must be accompanied by a courageous and intelligent effort to rid our nation and our churches, as well as the attitude of our peoples, of the encrusted barnacles of racial prejudice and discrimination.

I

It is not because the churches lack a knowledge of the situation that they were slow to develop positive and progressive action. The warning flags were raised both by some missionaries and African Christians for a long time. Nor is it because they lack a sense of dedication, or the insights necessary to motivate a new program. Certainly it has not been because of a lack of funds. The churches of America have been talking and planning strategy for a decade and the recent experiences of the religious crisis in Asia, from which we should have learned, still trouble our conscience and smolder in our hearts. The blame lies rather in the whole attitude of the West, the churches included, toward Africa as a "dark continent peopled with ignorant, superstitious, uncultured children." We have been acculturated by our own success in a prosperous country, conditioned by Europeans, and stymied by colonial control. Our whole society is involved and all of us must share some of the blame. Even the great Negro Protestant denominations in America have been no more aware of the tremendous forces taking shape on the continent and no more ready to deal with them or to take hold of opportunities for the church in Africa than any other denomination. In fact, it is fair to say that they have not been as creative and as effective as some of the predominantly white denominations.

Some of the faults can be specified: The paternalism that blinded us to the real problems and opportunities. The lack of appreciation for African cultural heritage and social customs. Pride in our own ways and methods that kept us from being receptive to African ideas and forced us to take utterly false positions against the African who talks back, expressing his own ideas and grievances. The failure of Christian laymen in business and government to bear witness to their faith. Our lack of contact with the rising African leaders who, for good or ill, must be the persons to be dealt with in the immediate future. Racial ideas and attitudes in ourselves that we have not submitted wholly to the discipline of Christ's ideal of brotherhood. When leaders, whether missionaries or others, are motivated by racial antagonism, snobbery, and superiority, they become far too small to help clothe the world with God's love. And finally the denominational division of the missionary effort that has never, and does not now allow, except in a very small degree, for the concentration of religious effort that the new Africa demands.

The situation is grave. The problems differ widely from place to place. The leap in time is great for Africans and also for us, but especially for those Africans who are just emerging from primitive fear and superstition. The African church is weak and its most serious need is capable, trained Christian leadership. Furthermore, Christian forces face two great challenges: the recrudescence of Islam, which has outgrown Christianity two to one in the past and now in many areas is exceeding it by almost eight converts to one. Secondly, Christian forces also face not only the rising secularism of the church's younger people and new leaders but, in addition, are threatened by the missionary zeal of communism that restlessly sows the tares of its nefarious ideas at every opportunity.

Nevertheless we venture to suggest some things that the church and missions must and can do without delay. The forces of history are neither deterred by time nor by the unreadiness on the part of peoples. Only a concerted, co-operative effort of all religious bodies of America can make possible the best utilization of our funds, make available our ablest personnel and our most effective resources for the strengthening of African church leadership. Most of our attempts have been too late, too little, and too divided. There can be no doubt of the fact that we can be both thankful and proud of the work Christian missions have done in Africa in the past, but when all is said and done, we must admit that our total contribution has been wholly inadequate. Only a gigantic effort will suffice, and we must remember that though church and mission co-operation on a broad scale naturally poses many difficult and complex problems, none of these is too great for true Christian spirit and the grace of God to overcome.

II

There is a most urgent need for re-examination of our over-all policy and strategy, both individually and collectively. Divided, our witness is so dissipated and fragmentary that we cannot successfully deploy our forces and make the best use of them. We find it increasingly difficult to meet the issues of the hour proposed by the new Governments, the rising political movements, the enemies of our faith, and the pressing urban problems created by rapid social change.

For example, the Christian Council of Kenya in 1954 desperately asked for aid from the churches of the world in order to undertake the task of rehabilitating the thousands of former Mau Mau followers. This was too great a task for its own resources. The spiritual recovery of these people was as important as economic recovery and political and social advance. They did receive some aid through the World Council of Churches, but most of their appeals in this country fell on deaf ears. The great outpouring of funds and personal resources, such as only a co-ordinated and total approach could have provided, were never forthcoming. Therefore we were not in a position to take advantage of a windfall of opportunity.

There are many things we can do better together by a co-ordinated effort than we can ever do alone. One of the great needs, not only of the church but of the nations of Africa, is for better communication. By this is meant the communication of the gospel to the people of Africa by the use of modern techniques, through the printed page, not only in their vernacular but even for those who can read French, English, and Portuguese, and also through the modern means of radio. Many Governments, particularly in French-speaking and British West Africa, have demonstrated the great effectiveness of the use of the radio through their information service programs. Almost all of these facilities have religious program time allotted by the Governments to the various religious groups.

One can be glad that the Sudan Interior Missions has been in the forefront of developing the communication of the gospel by the airways across all boundaries, but we are nevertheless chagrined that few churches have joined together in this method of evangelism by pooling their resources and personnel in a co-operative effort; for instance, in training Africans as the British Broadcasting Company has done, particularly in Sierra Leone, Ghana, and Nigeria. It would be tragic if each denomination began developing its own meager, separate efforts. This would be far more confusing than the present divisions.

Co-operation in this area might well inspire pilot projects for the Governments themselves to improve communication across Africa directly between contiguous countries. For example, to send a cable from Lomé in Togo to Accra in Ghana, a distance of less than two hundred miles, can be done for only a few hours a day. Even then the cable goes from Togo to Paris to London, then back to Accra. To send a letter takes several days, but one can fly the distance in twenty minutes or travel it by road in three and a half hours with a half-hour wait at the Volta River for the ferry. There will be many, of course, who say that this is not the problem of the church, but such people forget that Jesus' words, "I came that you might have life, and that more abundantly," refer not merely to the religious and moral life of man but to a totality of life that encompasses everything that affects the children of God. Happiness, security, progress, and cultural development are not ruled out of that abundant life he brings.

III

Therefore to meet the challenge of these times and minister to Africa's needs, the church must move boldly into a new program. Its first obligation must be to build up strong African churches that will be capable of meeting the present situation. We must help that church evolve a leadership adequate to the times. We must help to support, educate, and develop leaders who will become equal partners with the leaders of the churches in America and the missionaries or fraternal workers on the field. The Presbyterian Church of East Africa has only one college-trained, religious leader out of two hundred pastors and the proportion is about the same almost everywhere in

Africa. Of the nearly 2,500 students from Africa in educational institutions of the United States, less than 3 per cent are training for religious leadership. Our efforts to develop leadership training in theological seminaries in Africa, to provide institutions for better training of African pastors who will never go to college or university and hence not receive theological education at the seminary level, must be redoubled. Moreover, it is the duty and the responsibility of the churches in America to help to provide more graduate-level education for African Christian leaders in this country, as well as to enlarge seminary facilities of the highest intellectual quality on the African continent as the Theological Education Fund in Africa has already begun to do.

The surveys of training for the ministry in Africa, carried out in the 1950's by the International Missionary Council, have emphasized the needs for thorough post-ordination training in the churches of all regions of Africa, especially at the level of those pastors who never in their lifetime will be able to get through high school or college but are already in service. If this is necessary at such a level, how much more necessary is it to prepare pastors at the higher theological level. The momentous changes of political and social conditions in Africa face the ministry of the churches with a challenge that they are not now able to meet. The younger generation of Africans, both at home and abroad, feel that their pastors and religious leaders no longer are in touch with the dynamic forces shaping the present and the future. They are beginning to view the church as irrelevant to present-day events in Africa. Happily the uneducated pastors are eager and hungry for the training we can help to provide. A series of constructive, well-organized, and staffed theological institutes with short-duration refresher courses would do wonders for the church in Africa.

The church situation in Africa has been aggravated by

the rapid growth of the Separatist Movement among African Christians. This is a problem too little known in America. Dissatisfaction with some of the mission churches, the attitude of the missionaries themselves, the racial patterns of the church, especially in South Africa with its apartheid policy, the slowness of the mission boards to stand up to the colonial powers and to formulate a new policy have, since the turn of the century, been foremost among the reasons that have encouraged the Separatist churches. These have now grown to some fifteen hundred, especially in South, Central, and East Africa. Furthermore the problem has been compounded by the fact that the churches of America and their missions in Africa have shown no interest in these offshoot branches of Christians seeking the way according to their own lights. Even at present there are very few contacts between the regularly established mission churches and the Separatist groups and too few imaginative and compassionate steps toward reconciliation have been taken. More often than not the Separatists have been undisciplined and unwilling to co-operate and therefore have been ignored by the established churches, whom they equally ignore. Although the problem is complex and difficult and overlaid with serious emotions and hostilities, it should be possible through concerted action, Christian love and charity, and patient understanding to build some rapport with these groups and to help to convey to their younger generation of pastors and leaders a deeper understanding of the Christian faith and of their task. Christians everywhere must never weary of healing schisms in the body of Christ.

A highly significant way in which individual American Christians and local churches in this country could participate is to provide a small but meaningful theological library for every pastor consistent with the level of his training. Such a gift of books would not only serve the pastor well in his own personal growth and development but would help him in the development of a better understanding of his relationship to the new Africa and deepen his spiritual life intellectually.

Perhaps nothing is so important as the development and strengthening of an indigenous Christian leadership. In some African areas, the Church of England, the Roman Catholic Church, and a few Protestant churches have taken some farsighted steps in this direction, but everywhere else, too little is being done, and in some churches there has been little or no movement in this direction. Few Christian missions have raised Africans to positions of partnership at the level of administration and policy-making. An indigenous leadership, as the Communists recognize at the outset of their efforts everywhere, will remain when all else and all others have passed away. Communists are staking their future on African communists rather than European communists, because the former can move faster and more freely without the hostility which encumbers Europeans and Americans, whom Africans think of as foreigners allied with colonial control. African leaders do not have to prove the genuineness of their concern with African problems. Furthermore, they know the language. It is most damaging to the missionary movement that the labor and the political forces that have been at the center of the unfolding destiny of Africa in recent years have been led by Africans who largely received their first education in mission schools, while so very few Africans have come to similar leadership roles in the missions. It is therefore fair to ask why the missions have developed so few comparable leaders for the work of the Christian churches.

Only a strengthened, indigenous, African-led church can provide the moral and spiritual resources without which Africa's future will be chaotic and perhaps even disastrous. Up to now there is only a handful of trained social, welfare, and labor workers, or specialists in youth work, although the expanding urban centers, choked with misery and disorganized families, rampant with disease and moral degradation, lost young people swept up in the delinquent vacuum that always accompanies urbanization, have created social and religious problems of great magnitude. It is both our duty and our task to help the church in Africa develop an urban ministry with Christian social and welfare centers, an industrial evangelism, an adequate youth program, and an enlarged ministry in women's work. Only so will it be able to meet the grave social, family, and personal problems created by urbanization. In the final analysis, it will be the African church that will have to bear the burden of Africa's Christian future. But it should be the aim of the Christian church in America to help bring it to the place where it can do so.

IV

Much more attention must be given to the preparation of African women for leadership roles. Of the 2,500 African students in this country, far too few are women. But the problem must be worked on back at home before they attain college level, for while the adult woman is a very important part of the African society, the education and training of young women has lagged very far behind that of the males. Since no underdeveloped area can be lifted any higher than its women, it is imperative that we do as much as we can to develop programs along these lines. The women of Africa are ready for them and will not only take advantage of the opportunities but will make great use of the advancement in education. An enlightened womanhood in any society strengthens the social and moral fabric of that society. More serious consideration must also be given to the type and kind of education a pastor's wife should have. It may not be possible to make such training available on the same intellectual level as that of her husband, but help can be given consistent with her needs. In much of Africa the pastor's wife is the person of second importance in the local parish. Furthermore, she is the teacher and leader of other women. It is a very hopeful sign indeed when a large percentage of Africans coming to this country on grants provided by churches, secular organizations, educational institutions, and programs of the United States Government want to bring their wives in order that they may have some exposure to the dynamic forces of which they are a part.

The communists are working overtime to win awakening African youth and students, both in Africa and wherever they are studying abroad. They do not limit their expenditure of funds and organization of personnel to carry out this work to universities in Soviet-Bloc countries or in Russia itself. Wherever there are large numbers of students in any country, communist agents are at work in subtle ways, trying to take advantage of the minds and hearts of the people whom we are training for leadership roles in Africa. Consequently, one of the most demanding needs is a trained youth leadership in Africa at the high school and college level. There are certainly less than ten trained, experienced African church youth leaders in the whole continent. Consequently, in many areas the church and missions are no longer able to hold or influence the youth as they once did.

The youth of Africa are on the march. What they will find, where they will end, and whom they will follow will depend largely upon who works the hardest to win their loyalty, to educate, train, and inspire them, and who will identify with the African young people and their hopes for a better future. One of the most important things the churches can do immediately is to place in the field in Africa some of the ablest and most experienced youth workers it can loan for either long or short periods; and it should be the job of those loaned to work with the youth now, but even more to help provide training for an African youth leadership that will take over in their places as rapidly as possible. The preparation of leaders who can be partners with us in all fields of endeavor and eventually assume full responsibility so that we can become their assistants, should be high on the list of our priorities.

Fortunately the church neither lives, moves, nor advances by its executives, its boards, and its administrators alone. Their work is possible only to the extent that there is an enlightened, dedicated group of laymen who voluntarily accept the call of Christ in their hearts and give themselves to his service to do whatever they can, where they are, according to their knowledge of God's will. The largest tasks of the church on the African continent will not be undertaken by outstanding leaders or administrators but by the men and women in the pews. There is some vital and significant part that each one of them can play. If they do not take their places in the work of the church, that work will never be done.

There are five things which American laymen can do as their part in the Christian advance in Africa.

First, they can make themselves aware and knowledgeable of the forces reshaping the new Africa and of our relationship to it, and they can understand and help the whole church, as well as the nation, to realize that the Africans are our brothers and that the land of Africa is but one of the great branches of the family of God.

In the second place, from the vantage point of their own enlightenment they can prod their leaders to develop new, adventurous, and creative programs for which they will supply their sons and daughters as well as their means.

In the third place, there are so many more laymen than clergy and missionary personnel combined that if they would undertake to be friends with Africans in this country, the unlimited manpower and resources they would provide could give the church the gigantic lift it needs for the immediate future and multiply the efforts of the mission boards manyfold. They could work not only with students but with the leaders and officials who are increasingly coming here for short-term experience, and in addition they could adopt African schools, colleges, women's groups, youth organizations, social welfare agencies, and hospitals to supply books, medicines, equipment, materials, etc. There are now nearly one hundred organizations and agencies in addition to the regular church channels through which the laymen can work.

In the fourth place, and perhaps most important of all, laymen of skill in fields that urgently need personnel can offer themselves for service to missions, governments, secular or private agencies. In Canada a group of doctors, who were members of the United Church of Canada, was inspired by Operation Crossroads Africa. They began a Canadian Goodwill Mission program to get doctors in that country, who could afford to pay for their own transportation and finance themselves, to serve in hospitals, health clinics, medical centers, and other facilities on the continent of Africa. Similar plans have been developed in the Congo and elsewhere by individuals with religious motivation in the United States. Dr. McKinley Wiles, a Harlem physician, and his wife, a trained nurse, have gone to Africa at their own expense to serve Africa's medical needs all over the continent for three years without any thought of compensation. This couple went to Africa because they believe it to be their Christian duty. After similar voluntary service in Haiti with Dr. Mellon, a couple in New Canaan, Connecticut, both of whom are physicians, aroused their whole community and other doctors to share in their effort of voluntary medical service to Guinea. Surely, with a minimal effort but with careful advance planning, surveys on the field, consultation with African authorities with a view to immediate needs, and the acceptance of long-range opportunities—not emotionally charged, one-time operations—we could mount a medical witness that would do justice to the healing ministry of our Lord and bring health and strength to thousands upon thousands of God's darker children.

Fifth, laymen can bring the power of moral and religious influence upon Government policy both at home and abroad. Whether their impact changes anything or not is not the main issue. If their cause is right and they work with patience, tenacity, humility, and wisdom, their influence will not be lost. Christians are obligated to make their witness for God's sake, for righteousness' sake, and God's peoples' sake, even to the point of suffering and sacrifice. To these very ends, men and women stood against slavery in the early days of our history. In a more practicable way, the churches of America ought long ago to have had a well-organized and expertly staffed office in Washington and in New York near the United Nations to keep in contact with officials and events and to advise the churches and their members on the vital issues that affect the lives of people, the fortunes of nations, and the future of the world.

V

It must not be overlooked, however, that the greatest liabilities against the spread of the gospel in Africa are racial discrimination and segregation, whether in Africa, in Europe, or in the United States. The sin of racism is and will continue to be the most difficult handicap to overcome. Racism is a cancer within our society, our Christian institutions, and within ourselves as well as within the colonial structure. It is still the affliction of many of the individuals who represent the United States in Africa. Many Americans in Africa make very quick accommodation to European patterns of racism and then add to it some of their own American styles.

In the minds of the Africans, racism is identified with white people. White people are identified with Christianity. Communists, Moslems, and many of the secular leaders undercut the influence of African Christian leaders by charging that they are in league with those who perpetrate the crime of color prejudice and discrimination. On no other subject, save possibly eventual and complete independence, are Africans so greatly agitated and united as they are on their opposition to attitudes and patterns of racial discrimination. There is no greater hunger in Africa, other than freedom, than the hunger for acceptance, brotherhood, and human decency and dignity. Africa longs for the time when the personality of a man will not be violated, ignored, or limited on account of his race or color. Nor is there any greater fear among Africans coming to this country than the fear of the discrimination they have heard so much about before they come, and which more frequently than not, they experience while in this country.

Africans are not only concerned about racial attitudes toward themselves. They cannot have supreme confidence in us so long as they see the pattern of racial attitudes toward American Negroes that also backwashes upon them. They are deeply concerned that citizens of the United States, to whom they look for understanding and support, have been so slow to confront and overcome the race problem in our democracy. If we are to be true to the gospel of Jesus Christ, the churches and missions simply cannot evade this problem. It is not merely a question of the practical moves needed to win Africa or to hold back the nefarious hosts that seek to seduce Africa, it is a question of morality, of human decency, of Christian love, and the matching of our protestations with our deeds. The African, in this matter, may not demand the accomplishment of miracles overnight, but unless he sees some convincing and practical demonstration of our humility and willingness to eliminate the racist denial of the gospel we preach, he will turn in revulsion from us, if not against us. There is no escape from the necessity of clothing our lofty sentiments with deeds and making the church real, not alone by our confessions but also by our actions.

For Africa, the brightest or the darkest years lie just ahead. The outcome depends largely, if not wholly, on whether the Christian church can understand the implications of its faith, whether the laity of the church will yield to the will of God to serve where best they can, "as each bears his mild yoke." If the churches fail to understand and obey, they will not be able to provide the moral and spiritual basis upon which the African, who will claim leadership and succeed to power, can build a new Africa soundly and wisely. Whether they can act with Christian resourcefulness, speed, and power, and under the command of Christ to make disciples of all men by being true disciples themselves is the question upon which their destiny is poised.

Questions for Study and Discussion

Chapter I. The New Perspective on Africa

1. What are some of the popular impressions you have of Africa? In a small group try a "word association test," having the members write down impressions as they come to mind. Discuss the ideas, myths, and just plain misinformation we have somehow collected about Africa and its peoples.

2. What is the historical and social significance of the fact that America's involvement with Africa began with the slave trade?

3. What are the resources inherent in the gospel itself that contributed to the impact of Christian missions on Africa? How do these compare with the influence of the gospel in America and with the influence of communism and socialism upon Africans?

Chapter II. The Process of Cultural Revolution

1. What do you think was the reason for the tardiness of a positive American policy on Africa? Does this slowness of American reaction have anything to do with the attitudes of the American churches and their mission policies?

2. The author speaks of "the rediscovery of Africa by Western nations . . . and the discovery of the world by Africans." How can your own church participate in Africa's discovery of the world? What kind of world do Africans experience in your community?

3. What should be the attitude of African Christians toward the use of violence in the struggle for independence?

4. What is your opinion regarding the situation in the

Congo today? What role could the churches have played in that crisis?

5. Do you agree that people must be prepared for democracy and self-government and that to permit them to assume self-government before they are capable of handling it may be injurious to their best interests in the long run?

Chapter III. Forces Changing Africa Today

1. How would you assess the differences between the contributions of Islam and of Christianity to Africa? Will the positive influence of Christianity be lessened as the churches discontinue traditional missionary programs and turn over their work to indigenous African churches?

2. How important is it for Africans to become nationalistic in terms of self-consciousness and Pan-Africanism before they become internationalistic or world-minded?

3. Do you agree with the author that whatever we do in Africa must, in the final analysis, be for the "major benefit of Africans"? How does this square with "enlightened self-interest" which he also seems to support? Is altruism the only response to Africa that will have the purity and integrity that should characterize a "Christian policy"?

4. Do you agree that "Africans can deal more successfully with communism in their continent than anyone else"? What do you think of Robinson's analysis of the communist danger in Africa today?

Chapter IV. Rapid Changes Demand New Strategies

1. How can American foreign policy for Africa support and encourage the new nations in their search for independence and rapid social progress without appearing to be paternalistic and smugly charitable?

2. Should we rely chiefly upon direct aid to new African nations or utilize the channels of the UN or some other international agency? What differences would this make in our relations with Africans and our European allies?

3. Do you agree with the discussion of African neutralism?

Can this be a morally responsible position under present world conditions?

4. What do you think is the logic or illogic, or what are the advantages or disadvantages, of Africans and American Negroes identifying across national boundaries and making a common definition of their problems?

Chapter V. The Responsibility of American Christians

1. What should be the difference between the roles that the church and the state should play with regard to the future of Africa?

2. The author is critical of the ineffectiveness of the African missions of the great Negro denominations. What is the reason for this ineffectiveness and what should and can be done about it?

3. How can the churches help American Christian businessmen, students, diplomats, tourists, and other travelers to take part in a Christian witness to Africa?

4. Discuss and evaluate the projects described by the author such as the programs in communication, women's work, training ministers, and Operation Crossroads. What can your church do immediately as well as on a long-range basis about taking some share in a new, creative ministry to Africa?